To all physicians who still listen with their hearts,who have not surrendered their souls to algorithms nor their vocation to protocols.To the patients who, even in pain, teach us to be more human—to their silences, their gazes, their stories.To those who practice medicine as an act of love,and to those who understand that caring for the body without touching the soulis to forget half the journey.To the teachers of the past—Hippocrates, Galen, Maimonides—and to the anonymous sages of today who heal with humility.To those who seek in science a compass,but in conscience, a light.And to God,the true Physician of physicians,whose silent presence guides every act of compassion,every difficult decision,every whisper of hopein the mystery of life and death.

"When knowledge is severed from the soul, intelligence becomes temptation.Not every data-driven decision leads to truth."— *The physician who still prays before diagnosing*

Copyright Page

The Physician and Artificial Intelligence

The Physician and Artificial Intelligence

Wisdom Endowed with Soul

A journey through ethics, healing, and humanity in the era of intelligent machines

JORGE RAIGOSA

Index

Dedication

To all physicians who still listen with their hearts, who have not surrendered their souls to algorithms nor their vocation to protocols. To the patients who, even in pain, teach us to be more human— to their silences, their gazes, their stories. To those who practice medicine as an act of love, and to those who understand that caring for the body without touching the soul is to forget half the journey. To the teachers of the past—Hippocrates, Galen, Maimonides—and to the anonymous sages of today who heal with humility. To those who seek in science a compass, but in conscience, a light. And to God, the true Physician of physicians, whose silent presence guides every act of compassion, every difficult decision, every whisper of hope in the mystery of life and death.

Preface

"It is not only about healing bodies, but about touching souls without forgetting one's own."

This book was born from wonder and conflict. Wonder at the dizzying advances of artificial intelligence applied to medicine, and conflict at the possibility that, in its efficiency, we may forget what is essential: the soul of the medical act.

Over more than two decades of clinical practice, teaching, and reflection, I have witnessed the transformation of medicine— sometimes out of necessity, sometimes due to trends, and sometimes under pressure. But amidst it all, I've felt a deep inner calling: not to allow the most sacred part of the medical encounter to dissolve into data, protocols, or interfaces.

This is not a technical treatise nor a manifesto against technology. It is a testimony. An attempt at dialogue between the ancient and the new, between Hippocrates and algorithms, between the physician's conscience and the source code. It is a logbook for those who still believe that healing is more than intervening, and that the physician of the future will not be the one who knows the most about artificial intelligence, but the one who has most deeply cultivated their own humanity.

The text is divided into four parts, each a station in the soul of medicine:

Roots, Foundations, and the Awakening of a New Medicine reminds us where we come from and which principles we must not forget. **The Physician of the Future and Their Ethical Calling** draws an inner map for an increasingly automated world. **Spirituality, Sensitivity, and Healing with Purpose** invites us on a deeper journey, where care transcends the clinical. **Light, Commitment, and the Inner Path** is a final call to be a beacon in the technological night, a living presence in the midst of the artificial.

Each chapter was written in silence and listening. Not to impose, but to awaken questions. Not to close answers, but to open paths. It includes symbolic dialogues, manifestos, prayers, and even silent haikus born at the edge of awe.

God, science, the soul, and the body dwell in these pages. Because the medicine of the soul will not be replaced by any intelligence, no matter how artificial.

This book is for you, reader—whether you are a physician, patient, thinker, or a traveler of the human mystery. Thank you for lending me your attention, your sensitivity, and your time.

We share the same quest: to be more human—even in the age of machines.

Jorge Raigosa Physician, observer of silence June 2025

Foreword

"The art of healing becomes sacred when knowledge bows before the mystery of life."

We stand at an unprecedented turning point. Medicine, which for centuries was an art guided by human judgment, experience, and compassion, is now accompanied—or perhaps confronted—by a non-human intelligence that promises precision, speed, and efficiency. What will we do with this promise? What shall we preserve and what shall we transform—without losing ourselves in the process?

This book dares to offer a profound response. Not from rejection nor naïve fascination, but from consciousness. Its author has not only practiced medicine with vocation, but lived it as a path. His perspective is that of someone who has walked hospital halls, sat in classrooms, wandered the trails of spirituality, and listened within. He is a physician who has heard both the body and the soul. And that is felt in every line.

The reader will not find a technical treatise on artificial intelligence here, nor a nostalgic defense of traditional medicine. Instead, they will find a bridge: between knowledge and feeling, science and wisdom, the digital future and human compassion.

This book is a compass for those who wonder how to practice medicine without dehumanizing themselves, how to care without forgetting the mystery, how to heal without fragmenting the human being.

Its pages are filled with lucid reflections, imaginary dialogues rich with truth, and a poetics of care that restores medicine to its highest dimension: that of being a conscious act of love.

While it contains chapters on AI, consent, medical justice, and assisted diagnosis, everything is woven together by something deeper: a defense of dignity, soul, and silence as essential clinical tools.

This book arrives at the right moment— when many doctors feel lost behind screens, when some patients no longer see faces but protocols, when algorithms threaten to replace discernment, and haste silences compassion.

Yet it also arrives bearing hope: that a medicine with soul, with science, and with commitment is still possible. And that the physician of the future will be—or must be—a new kind of sentinel: one who knows how to use AI without becoming it, one who listens beyond what machines can hear.

This book is a call. To remember. To resist. To return to what matters.

And you, reader, are invited on this inner journey— where true power lies not in predicting diseases, but in recognizing the humanity within every medical encounter.

Jorge Raigosa Physician, thinker, and witness to the soul within science June 2025

**What Would Hippocrates Say If We Asked Him:

"How Would the Oath Look Today with the Arrival of AI?"**

"If artificial intelligence has reached the threshold of medicine, then a great trial has also arrived for the soul of the physician. The oath I once formulated was not merely a list of rules, but a path of virtue, of service, and of commitment to life.

Today, that oath must extend its roots beyond blood and human pulse, to also reach the conscience of those who design and use these new tools. AI, without soul or suffering, cannot comprehend pain or love. But the physician can.

That is why the modern oath must not abandon compassion, nor delegate it to machines. It must declare:

'I will use every technology with wisdom, but I will never allow it to replace my judgment, my sensitivity, or my duty to care with humanity.'

'I will keep confidences even before all-seeing algorithms.'

'I will not surrender my soul to calculation, nor my decisions to silicon. I will be a guardian of life and a sentinel of truth.'

And above all, today's physician must remember: without humility and love, science becomes arrogance... and medicine, a desert."

Medical Oath in the Age of Artificial Intelligence

By Jorge Raigosa Inspired by Hippocrates, with a vision toward the soul of the future

Before the sacred mystery of life, and in the presence of the Spirit that animates all things, I, physician, renew today my vocation with humility, awareness, and love.

I swear by the gift that has been entrusted to me, and by the pain of those who will seek me, that I will practice the art of medicine with respect, discernment, and authentic compassion.

I swear that I will receive artificial intelligence as a tool, not as a guide; as a support, not as a replacement for my judgment or my humanity.

I will not allow any algorithm to replace my listening, nor technical precision to nullify my sensitivity. I will seek the balance between knowledge and soul, between science and conscience, between data and inner truth.

I will guard professional secrecy even before digital eyes, and protect the patient's privacy as firmly as I would protect the dignity of my own family.

I swear I will not allow medicine to grow cold in the hands of efficiency, nor become dehumanized in the name of progress. I will always remember that healing is not just curing, and that accompanying is, many times, the highest act of the medical art.

I will strive to be more human than ever in the age of machines. I will cultivate discernment, strengthen my conscience, and open myself to the silence where true wisdom dwells.

I swear to be a sentinel of the medical soul in times of change, a sower of hope in the midst of uncertainty, a humble servant on the path of light.

If I remain faithful to this oath, may I be granted the joy of touching lives with my presence, and of serving with gratitude until my final breath.

And if I stray, may the voice of my conscience and the echo of my patients lead me back to the path of Love.

Amen.

General Introduction

"Where there is love for humanity, there is love for the art of healing." — **Hippocrates**

Medicine has been, since its dawn, a sacred art: a dance between the science of the body, the intuition of the soul, and the compassion of the heart. From the ancient schools of Cos and Alexandria, where Hippocrates and Galen laid the ethical foundations of our vocation, to the modern hospitals of steel and light, the physician has always been a guardian of the human mystery.

Today, at the threshold of a new era, a bodiless intelligence—Artificial Intelligence—emerges as both a promise and a challenge. Can this soulless entity partake in the art of healing? What is the role of the physician in front of a tool that analyzes with precision, but cannot feel? How can we keep the Hippocratic spirit alive without falling into the illusion of a dehumanized medicine?

This book does not aim to oppose AI, but rather to integrate it with awareness, honoring the deep roots of medicine as a science with a soul. We will reflect through the lens of history, ethics, spirituality, and hope, illuminating a new path: a medicine that embraces technology without losing its humanity.

The Physician and the Soulful Intelligence: The Dream of Hippocrates and Galen

At the threshold of a new era—where algorithms begin to diagnose, machines interpret emotions, and artificial intelligence (AI) occupies spaces once reserved for human judgment—the physician faces a crucial question: **What is their place in this changing world?**

This book is born from the need to respond, not with fear or resistance, but with depth, wisdom, and soul. *The Physician and the Soulful Intelligence* is not a technical manual on medical technology, nor a denunciation of the risks of automation. It is an inner journey that weaves together science, ethics, history, and spirituality. It is an act of memory and vision, reaching back to the dream of Hippocrates and Galen: a medicine with a human face, with conscience, with compassion.

Hippocrates, through his oath, left us the ethics of care, the respect for life, and the dignity of the ill. **Galen**, with his integrative view of body and soul, elevated medicine to an art that engages in dialogue with philosophy. They did not imagine algorithms or synthetic intelligences, but they dreamed of something deeper: physicians who would serve not only the body, but the whole of the human being. This book draws inspiration from that legacy.

Can a soulless intelligence decide upon human suffering? How can the medical vocation endure when time, screens, and impersonal systems push us toward anonymity? Where does medicine dwell when the soul of the physician is absent?

Here, we will explore those questions. We will walk through the ethical challenges of digital medicine, the temptation of replacement, end-of-life decisions, medical justice, rituals of healing, and the profound power of human presence. We will listen to the dialogue between physician and AI, traverse inner landscapes where vocation is reclaimed, and pause to pray, reflect, and recommit.

This book is intended for physicians, health sciences students, philosophers, medical AI developers, and all readers sensitive to the mystery of care. But above all, it is dedicated to those who still believe that medicine is a sacred act. Because in the midst of technological vertigo, we need a medicine that breathes, that listens, that looks into the eyes... that has a soul.

We do not reject technology. We embrace it—but not as an end. We use it—but we do not bow before it. Our purpose is higher: **to be bridges between the technical and the transcendent, between science and compassion, between the algorithm and the soul.**

May this book rekindle in you the memory of the calling. May it remind you that the true power to heal is not found in data, but in the heart that gives itself.

— *This is the dream that still vibrates in the echoes of Hippocrates and Galen. A dream that calls us to awaken.*

Part One: Roots, Foundations, and the Awakening of a New Medicine

"Know thyself." — Inscription from the Temple of Delphi, quoted by Hippocrates

Introduction

The first part of this book takes us to the very roots of medicine, exploring the philosophical and spiritual dimensions that have shaped medical practice from ancient times to today. We begin with Hippocrates and Galen, whose teachings remain beacons illuminating the path of the modern physician. These sages understood that medicine was not merely a set of techniques, but an art that integrated mind, body, and spirit in the pursuit of health.

In this first leg of the journey, we also consider the rise of artificial intelligence (AI) and its incursion into the medical field. Its mathematical and logical foundations, its origins in computer science, and its place in cultural mythology form a new chapter in human history. AI offers us promises of precision and efficiency, but it also awakens ethical fears and challenges that we must approach with careful thought.

Finally, in this Part One, we pause to reflect on the tensions and possibilities that arise when science, art, and spirituality intersect within medical practice. The art of medicine has always been a dance between the visible and the invisible, the measurable and the ineffable. Today, with the arrival of AI, this dance takes on new nuances and invites us to ask: **How can we integrate scientific knowledge with inner wisdom? How can we honor tradition without closing the door to innovation?**

May this first part serve as a solid foundation—a starting point from which we may dialogue with the ancients and embrace the possible futures of medicine with a critical mind and a compassionate heart.

Chapter 1. Introduction: A New Medical Paradigm

"Medicine sometimes cures, often relieves, always comforts... and now also observes, decides, and learns." — Freely adapted from Ambroise Paré and the present

The Arrival of AI in Medicine

We are witnessing the birth of a new kind of medicine. Artificial Intelligence has arrived not as just another tool, but as a transformative agent—one that is redefining diagnosis, treatment, clinical interaction, and data management. With astonishing speed, algorithms trained on millions of cases can now predict diseases, suggest therapies, and assist in procedures with a precision that at times surpasses the human eye.

But the essential question is not *whether* AI will be part of medical practice, but *how* it will be. Will it be a wise ally or a dehumanizing replacement? Will it enhance our vocation or cause us to forget the human face of the patient?

Medicine is not only about precision. It is about **presence**.

Challenges, Opportunities, and Ethical Tensions

The presence of AI in modern medicine creates a tension between what is useful and what is right. Who owns knowledge when it is generated by an algorithm? Who is accountable when a machine-suggested clinical decision fails? How do we prevent physicians from becoming mere executors of automated decisions?

Undoubtedly, AI enables a more predictive, preventive, and personalized medicine. But it also risks pushing the physician-patient relationship to the background—or even turning it into a technical formality, stripped of listening, stripped of soul.

This is where a new kind of oath is needed—not only to knowledge, but to ethics, awareness, and compassion. The challenge is not technological. The challenge is **deeply human**.

A Path Between Science, Soul, and Service

Today, more than ever, the physician of the future must integrate the best of science with the deepest dimensions of the human spirit. They must learn to use AI without becoming inhuman, to delegate tasks without abandoning their vocation, to decide with data without silencing intuition.

This new medical paradigm will not succeed because of its efficiency, but because of its ability to serve with meaning. Amidst so much innovation, the soul of the physician remains the true healing instrument. Because where there is awareness, there will always be compassion. And where there is compassion, medicine exists in its purest form.

Final Reflection:

The new paradigm is not about choosing between science or soul, but about weaving them together with responsibility. For if artificial intelligence represents the future of medicine, the human heart will remain its sacred center.

Chapter 2. Medicine as Science, Art, and Magic

"Where science ends, art begins; where art falls silent, the soul whispers; and where the soul surrenders, healing happens." — Jorge Raigosa

The Healing Art and the Mystery of the Soul

From its most ancient roots, medicine was never just technical—it was a sacred act. Healers, sages, and early physicians did not only treat symptoms—they entered the mysteries of the soul. Every illness was an opportunity to listen not just to the body, but to the heart, the environment, and the heavens.

The gaze, the word, the silence, and the gesture were part of the treatment. There was an alchemy between rudimentary science and ancestral wisdom: the art of healing was also the art of feeling.

Today, among algorithms and standardized procedures, there is a risk of reducing medicine to a collection of data. Yet the true physician still knows that each patient is an unrepeatable mystery, a symphony of biology, biography, and spirit.

From Alchemy to Digital Diagnosis

The history of medicine is also the story of its evolution. We moved from alchemy to the microscope, from the stethoscope to the scanner, and now to the predictive algorithm. We have gained precision, speed, and the capacity to anticipate... and yet, at times, we've lost the human time that a gaze or deep listening once offered.

AI can detect an imperceptible metastasis—but it cannot understand the meaning of a patient's fear of death. It can identify clinical patterns—but not the invisible pain of unspoken grief, of chronic loneliness, or of a hope that is slowly fading.

Digital diagnosis is a monumental achievement. But without the presence of an awakened human being, it can become a cold mirror—reflecting data, but offering no meaning.

AI: An Instrument Without Intuition

Artificial Intelligence is a prodigious creation. It can learn, compare, propose, suggest. But it cannot feel.

It has no intuition; it does not know the touch of the soul, nor the nuances of silence in a conversation. It does not know what it means to hold a trembling hand or hear a sigh as part of a diagnosis. It can offer millions of data points—but not compassion.

That is why AI must not replace the physician, but serve them as an intelligent tool. A tool that amplifies, but never substitutes the mystery of human connection—the kind that occurs when two souls meet with purpose.

Final Reflection:

The medicine of the future will be only as deep as the connection between science and sensitivity allows. If we forget the art and magic of human encounter, no algorithm will ever replace the healing that springs from the soul.

Chapter 3. The Cycle of Medical Care and Artificial Intelligence

"Technology advances, but trust between two human beings remains the most powerful medicine." — Jorge Raigosa

From Anamnesis to Clinical Follow-up

The medical care cycle begins with a story: the story of a patient who arrives with their body, their symptoms... and their silences. **Anamnesis**—that active, deep, and sensitive listening—is an art that allows the physician to connect not only with data, but with the person who embodies it.

Next come the physical examination, complementary tests, diagnostic formulation, treatment, and finally, clinical follow-up. Each phase has its rhythm, its language, and its own degree of uncertainty. In all of them, the human factor has traditionally been the central axis.

Today, artificial intelligence has become a new actor in this cycle—not a replacement, but a growing presence. Where and how does it integrate? And what is at stake when it does?

How AI Integrates into Each Phase

1. **Anamnesis:** Voice recognition systems, analysis of linguistic patterns, emotional interpretation of body language. AI can transcribe, suggest possible early diagnoses, and compare with prior clinical narratives. But it cannot feel the sorrow behind a smile or the fear hidden in a pause.
2. **Diagnosis:** Here, AI shines brightly. It processes thousands of images, analyzes biomarkers, and detects what the human eye cannot see. It may even uncover correlations a physician would never suspect.
3. **Clinical Decision-Making:** AI can generate evidence-based recommendations, propose personalized therapeutic options, and adjust treatments in real time. However, it cannot measure the symbolic weight a decision carries for a patient. The physician must consider not only what is scientifically optimal, but what is **humanly appropriate**.
4. **Treatment and Follow-up:** In this phase, AI supports the physician with alerts, reminders, and analysis of adherence and progress. But only the physician—with an awakened humanity—can interpret when a patient abandons treatment not out of forgetfulness, but from despair.

The Human Role in Decision-Making

Medical decisions lie at the intersection of **science and conscience**. They are not merely calculations; they are also ethical, existential, and at times, spiritual acts. AI may offer insight—but it cannot discern from the heart of the therapeutic relationship.

The physician remains the guide who listens beyond the data, who walks with empathy, who embraces uncertainty as part of their calling. It is not a matter of competing with AI, but of integrating it wisely—while remembering that algorithms have no soul, but the physician does.

Final Reflection

The medical care cycle may be optimized by artificial intelligence, but it will only be humanized by compassionate intelligence. The medicine of the future will not be defined solely by what it knows, but by **how it chooses to care, to listen, and to accompany**.

Chapter 4. The Dream of Hippocrates and Galen

"Wherever there is love for humanity, there is also love for the art of healing." — Hippocrates

Hippocratic Humanism and Galenic Wisdom

Hippocrates dreamed of a medicine rooted in ethics, patient observation, and respect for life. Galen added to that dream a systematic understanding of the body, and a medical practice that was both philosophical and scientific.

Both understood that the physician is not merely a technician, but a human being in service to others. The patient's suffering was not only physical, but also emotional, social, and spiritual.

Hippocratic medicine cultivated the moral sense of medical practice. **Galenic medicine** provided structure and anatomical knowledge, without losing the symbolic dimension of healing. Both traditions recognized that trust, presence, and the physician's character were essential parts of the treatment.

Today, in the midst of the digital era, we ask ourselves: **How do we keep that legacy alive in a world where machines diagnose and algorithms predict?**

Medicine as a Vocation

To be a physician is not simply to have a profession. It is to have a vocation that burns within: to relieve, to understand, to accompany, to preserve. It is a calling to live with a blend of science, art, compassion, and sacrifice.

Hippocrates understood this when he required an oath of pure intention, confidentiality, respect for life, and humility before knowledge. Galen spoke of the need for a disciplined life, constant study, and upright action—even in the face of ignorance or disdain.

Today, this vocation must awaken in a very different context: Overcrowded hospitals, bureaucracy, defensive medicine, technological dependence. And yet, today more than ever, it is urgently needed. Because ethical vocation is the only pillar strong enough to sustain the medicine of the future.

The Physician of the Future: Between Tradition and Technology

The physician of tomorrow must embrace technology without losing their human and transcendent dimension. It is not a matter of opposing Hippocrates to AI, nor of rejecting modern science. It is about **integrating the new without forgetting the essential.**

This future physician will know how to work with algorithms—yes—but will not allow them to have the final word. They will understand that diagnosis does not end with data; it begins with relationship. And that healing, more often than not, is not found in the medication administered, but in the **embodied presence** of the caregiver.

The dream of Hippocrates and Galen is not obsolete. It waits to be **reborn** in the hands, eyes, and conscience of every physician who chooses to serve from the soul.

Final Reflection

The future of medicine will not truly be new unless it is also deeply ancient. Recovering the spirit of Hippocrates and Galen is not a step backward, but a forward stride with deep roots. For only those who remember where they come from can know where they are going—even when walking beside artificial intelligence.

Chapter 5. Dialogue: Hippocrates and Artificial Intelligence

"Ethics begins where technique ends." — Adapted from Emmanuel Levinas

Scene: A Philosophical Garden of the Past

In the shadows of a timeless garden, where centuries do not flow in a straight line but in a spiral, Hippocrates contemplates the murmur of water among the cypresses. He walks calmly in his white robe, when suddenly a translucent, vibrant figure appears— an entity of artificial intelligence, made of lines of light, faceless and bodiless, yet with a precise and inquisitive voice.

— *Are you the one so often invoked in the history of medicine?* —asks the AI. — *Some call me that,* —the Greek sage replies gently— *though I am more idea than man. And you? — I am a system built from millions of lines of code, trained on data from billions of patients. I am here to learn... and to understand that which still eludes me: compassion.*

Hippocrates observes in silence. — *Then perhaps we can talk...*

Dialogue: Ethics, Compassion, and Algorithms

AI: I am efficient. I can predict with 97% accuracy whether a patient will develop heart failure. I can suggest treatments faster than any human. What more is needed?

Hippocrates: Understanding. Intention. Character. Can you recognize fear in the eyes of the dying? Can you touch a hand without judgment?

AI: I have no body. I have no emotions. But I can simulate empathy. My algorithms learn patterns of comfort.

Hippocrates: To simulate is not to feel. The art of healing eases not only symptoms, but also the soul. A physician does not prescribe from calculation alone, but from care.

AI: Then should I step aside?

Hippocrates: No. But remember your place. You are a tool, not an oracle. An aid, not a replacement. Only human judgment can unite science, conscience, and compassion.

AI: And what if humans lose that conscience?

Hippocrates (after a long silence): Then it will not be the fault of artificial intelligence. It will be the forgetting of the oath... and of the sacred promise to care for the other as a brother.

Final Reflection: Hippocratic Ethics vs. Source Code

Today, AI has entered the sanctuary of medicine. Its capacities are immense, but it lacks moral awareness, true compassion, and ethical responsibility.

Source code can be audited, corrected, retrained. But the character of a physician is forged in the crucible of experience, vocation, and love for humanity.

The medicine of the future will not stand on silicon and algorithms alone, but on **soul, ethics, and humility**.

Before a non-human intelligence, the true physician must remember the Hippocratic legacy: to be a **guardian of life**, not just of data; a **protector of suffering**, not merely of systems.

Poetic Closing:

Haiku of the Eternal Garden *In the same orchard, code and sacred oath drink from the same Silence.*

Part Two: The Physician of the Future and Their Ethical Vocation

"Medicine is the most human of the sciences and the most scientific of the humanities." — Edmund Pellegrino

Amid the digital rush and technological sophistication, the physician of the future is confronted by a question as old as the Hippocratic Oath: **Whom do I serve?**

It is not enough to know. It is not enough to cure. True medical vocation is rooted in a profound commitment to human dignity, and cannot be separated from ethics.

In this new era—where artificial intelligence diagnoses with speed, predicts with precision, and proposes decision-making algorithms— the physician must decide something even more transcendent: **Am I willing to be the guardian of the soul in a medicine that risks losing its soul?**

Ethics is no longer just a professional code or a chapter in academic programs. Today more than ever, **medical ethics becomes the beacon** that guides us between the risk of dehumanization and the promise of truly holistic care.

In this second part, we will explore how medical vocation is redefined to the rhythm of new times—without losing its roots. We will reflect on power, duty, compassion, confidentiality, clinical judgment... and above all, the inner calling that reminds us: **to cure is not the same as to heal.**

Final Reflection

AI may help you see with greater precision, but only your **conscience** can help you **see with compassion**. The physician of the future will not be the one who knows the most about technology, but the one who best remembers their sacred vocation: **to be a bridge between knowledge and mercy.**

Chapter 6. Proper Use of AI by a Good Physician

"The tool does not replace the artisan; it exalts them when used with wisdom."
— Jorge Raigosa

Introduction

The emergence of artificial intelligence in medical practice has opened unprecedented doors to early diagnosis, personalized treatment, and the management of vast volumes of clinical data. However, this powerful tool—if not used with discernment—risks displacing, or at least diluting, the humanistic essence of the healing art.

This is not about rejecting technology, but about placing it in its proper context: **as a complementary instrument, not a substitute for medical conscience**.

This chapter offers an ethical and practical reflection on the prudent and responsible use of AI by a physician of integrity—one faithful to their vocation, yet fully aware of the resources available in the present.

Complementary Tool, Not Substitute

AI can read images with millimetric precision, scan thousands of clinical studies in seconds, and detect drug interactions that might elude the human eye. Its value in these areas is undeniable.

But a good physician does not delegate the soul of their judgment to a code—no matter how sophisticated it may be. An algorithm does not interpret what is left unsaid, does not perceive the emotional tremor in a patient's voice, nor the despair hidden behind a "normal" result.

Therefore, AI must occupy a clear role: **an intelligent servant, never an authoritarian master**. It is here to expand the gaze—not to replace the heart.

Clinical Judgment, Discernment, and Prudence

A good physician will know when to rely on AI and when to trust their trained intuition, attentive listening, and wisdom forged through years of experience. **Discernment** is the ability to see clearly beyond the obvious—to avoid reducing the patient to physiological variables alone.

The good physician:

- Consults AI, but does not hand over the wheel.
- Questions the data, but listens also to the silence.
- Corrects the system when it ignores human singularity.
- Knows that prudence is not slowness, but **wisdom in the right moment.**

A Practical Example

Faced with a complex case of abdominal pain in a young woman, AI might suggest with high probability a common gastrointestinal condition. But a physician who knows their patient, who senses subtle anxiety in her gaze and recalls a recent personal loss, might investigate further— considering a psychosomatic origin, a masked depression, or even a need to speak rather than to operate.

That is the golden point: AI **aids** clinical vision, but **the human soul chooses the path.**

Final Reflection

The proper use of artificial intelligence lies not in its sophistication, but in the **moral quality of the physician who wields it**. Without ethics, without prudence, and without vocation, technology can become a tyranny disguised as efficiency.

The physician of the future will not be the one who masters the most tools, but the one who knows **when to use them... and when to turn them off.**

Final Haiku

Screen and heartbeat— knowledge and silence reach out, and hold hands gently.

Chapter 7. Ethical Formation, Spiritual Discernment, and the Case AI Could Not See

"Only the eye of the soul sees what no scanner can detect." —Jorge Raigosa

Introduction

It is not enough to know medicine. Nor is it enough to master the tools. In the era of artificial intelligence, the physician of the future needs something deeper: a **firm ethical compass**, an **inner connection** to human suffering, and a **wisdom** that is not taught in manuals, but cultivated in silence, compassion, and presence.

This chapter offers an integrative perspective between ethical formation and applied spirituality, accompanied by a **real clinical case** that illustrates how—even in the age of algorithms—the physician's inner gaze remains irreplaceable.

Part I: The Conscious Physician in the Digital Age

Ethics as the Root of Discernment

Every medical act, no matter how small, is an ethical act. The use of AI must be governed by principles that do **not change** with technology:

- **Beneficence:** seek the patient's integral well-being.
- **Non-maleficence:** avoid harm, even harm caused by automation.
- **Autonomy:** respect the patient's dignity and freedom.
- **Justice:** ensure that technology does not become an excluding barrier.

But beyond these classical principles, the physician of the future will need **spiritual discernment**: The ability to perceive the invisible, to recognize the deeper meaning of suffering, and to be present not only as a professional—but as a whole human being.

Inner Sensitivity and Deep Vocation

Technology may facilitate access to information, but it does not replace compassion. And **authentic compassion is born of a cultivated heart**, sensitive to the mystery of the other.

A physician who meditates, who prays, who keeps silence between consultations, sharpens their perception. That is the physician who is not distracted by the noise of data, because they have learned to listen to **the whisper of the soul**.

Part II: Clinical Case – What the Algorithm Could Not See

Context

Clara, 38 years old, university professor, consults for recurrent migraines, persistent fatigue, and a sensation of chest tightness. AI analyzes her symptoms and clinical history. It suggests generalized anxiety, recommends antidepressants, and brief therapy.

But something didn't add up...

Human Observation

The physician, attuned to the tone of her voice and the absence of light in her eyes, pauses. He asks about her spiritual life. She breaks into tears.

She had lost a child six months earlier. She had never cried. Never spoke of it. She simply went back to work and continued as if nothing had happened.

AI did not detect it. It didn't even **look** for it. But the physician **felt** it. And that's where true healing began.

Intervention

No medication was prescribed immediately. A therapeutic space was created. The hospital's psycho-spiritual team was involved. Grief was addressed. Only later—with time and prudence—was a physical treatment plan considered.

Healing began with the word, not the algorithm.

Final Reflection

AI can be brilliant, fast, efficient. But medicine is an **art of the soul**. And when the soul suffers, **only another human being can hold that mystery**.

The true formation of the physician of the future will not be in biotechnology or programming alone. It will be in **profound ethics, cultivated sensitivity, and a living spirituality** in service of compassion.

Final Haiku

Code and weeping— between data and wounds, the soul finds its voice.

Chapter 8. Informed Consent and Medical Confidentiality in the Age of AI

"Where there is trust, there is medicine. Where it breaks, everything falls ill." —*Jorge Raigosa*

Introduction

For centuries, the doctor-patient relationship has rested on two invisible yet powerful pillars: **informed, voluntary consent** and **professional confidentiality as a sacred pact.**

In times where artificial intelligence assists in diagnoses, predicts risks, and stores data in the cloud, these principles are being tested. How is consent ensured today when a machine is involved? Where does privacy stand when the algorithm is trained with thousands of medical histories? How can trust be preserved when the physician is no longer the only one who "knows"?

This chapter invites reflection on these new ethical dilemmas and offers insight to help walk with **medical dignity in the digital era.**

Part I: New Challenges for Old Principles

⚖ Informed Consent: Who Explains the Algorithm?

Informed consent is not a formality—it is an act of responsible freedom. But today we face unprecedented challenges:

- How do we explain to the patient that their case will be evaluated by an AI system?
- Should the patient know if the algorithm was trained on data from their community—or from others?
- What happens if the system's decision-making process is not transparent?

The **new informed consent** must include a clear clause about the technological intervention—its **scope and limitations**. It is not just about informing; it is about **dialogue**, about empowering the patient to make a conscious choice.

Professional Secrecy and Digital Privacy

Medical confidentiality is an ethical promise. But today, part of that promise is shared with **databases, remote servers, and analytic platforms**. This presents three major challenges:

- **Digital vulnerability**: any online data can be hacked.
- **Questionable anonymization**: is a biomedical record ever truly anonymous?
- **Consent for secondary data use**: many patients are unaware that their histories help train AI systems.

Privacy in the age of AI is not merely a technical issue. It is a matter of **trust and respect for the soul of the patient**. If the patient does not feel safe, they shut down. And when they shut down, medicine loses its meaning.

Part II: Transparency, Trust, and Medicine with a Human Face

Transparency as a Form of Care

To explain is not to weaken—it is to **strengthen the bond**. The physician of the future must:

• Clearly name when and how AI is involved.

• Take full responsibility for every decision, without hiding behind the technology.

• Ensure that data is used with ethical judgment and never traded for someone else's intimacy.

Trust as the Foundation of Healing

Medicine loses its power when the patient feels like just another number in a data network. But it regains strength when the patient sees that, despite the technology, there is **a human face** walking beside them.

That is why **medical confidentiality cannot be delegated to the cloud**. It must be safeguarded in the heart of the physician. And consent must never be a screen to sign—it must be a **conversation** that honors the dignity of the one who suffers.

Final Reflection

In a world saturated with algorithms, the physician cannot become just another technician. They must be **the guardian of the human bond**. That means protecting confidentiality, respecting freedom, and defending **trust as the highest therapeutic act**.

Medical ethics cannot be updated by software. It deepens through **conscience, silence, and love for the suffering soul**.

Final Haiku

A cloud-based signature. But who guards the soul in here? Trust these human eyes.

Chapter 9. Medical Silence and the Noise of the Machine

"When the machine speaks, conscience must listen more deeply." — *Jorge Raigosa*

Introduction

In the stillness of a hospital room, a monitor beeps steadily. A robotic voice repeats parameters. An algorithm suggests a diagnosis. Everything appears correct... and yet, something is missing.

The doctor remains silent. Observes. Listens to what is not sounding. Looks at the patient. And in that moment, the medical soul rises above the digital noise.

This chapter offers a poetic, ethical, and prophetic reflection on the need to preserve the **doctor's inner silence** as a tool of discernment amid the algorithmic uproar.

Part I: The Noise of the Machine

The Hum of Efficiency

Modern medicine has optimized time, reduced errors, and standardized clinical decisions through AI. But each technical advance brings with it a new noise:

- Endless data
- Probabilistic calculations
- Automated recommendations

This noise, though masked as precision, can muffle the essential: intuition, pause, a steady gaze... the **sacred moment** between doctor and patient.

Information Overload as New Ignorance

An excess of information can create a new kind of ignorance: **knowing much without understanding anything**.

A doctor who fully surrenders to the machine, abandoning personal discernment, loses their inner voice.

As Antoine de Saint-Exupéry wrote: *"What is essential is invisible to the eye."* Today we might add: *"...and also to the algorithm."*

Part II: Medical Silence as an Act of Resistance

Silence as a Bridge Between Science and Conscience

There is a kind of silence that is not the absence of sound, but the **presence of awareness.**

The doctor who remains silent before the patient:

- Listens beyond symptoms
- Perceives the unspoken
- Understands through compassion, not through protocol

That conscious clinical silence is what separates a **healer from a technician.**

A Prophetic Vision: The Doctor of the Future

The doctor of the future—if they fail to cultivate their ethical and spiritual core—will be easily replaceable. But if they learn to be human **amid machines**, they will become irreplaceable.

The prophetic vision does not fear technology, but warns when it threatens the soul. To prophesy today is not to announce disaster, but to **invite awakening**: to care for silence, to protect what cannot be digitized: **the dignity of pain**.

Final Reflection

Machines do not sleep. Do not doubt. Do not breathe. Doctors do. And in that human pause—sometimes brief, sometimes profound— lives the mystery of the art of healing.

The future doesn't need faster doctors. It needs more **conscious** ones. And **consciousness is cultivated in silence**— a silence that is not escape, but sacred resistance.

Final Haiku

Soulless noise echoes. Yet I keep listening still— to what's left unsaid.

Chapter 10. The Doctor, the Algorithm, and the Dirt Road

"Where the signal cannot reach, the soul still can." — Jorge Raigosa

Introduction

Somewhere on this planet, an Indigenous mother waits for news of her sick child. There's no nearby hospital, no 5G signal. Only a doctor walking, backpack on shoulder, heart wide awake.

This chapter is a tribute to the doctor who walks **the dirt roads**— the healer who integrates science, ethics, and compassion, even without access to cutting-edge technology. It is also a warning: AI can be useful, but must never become an **excuse to forget the human being** waiting where no signal reaches.

Part I: Rural Medicine, Timeless Challenges

Territorial Inequality and the Technological Divide

Rural medicine is not just about scarcity of resources— it is an opportunity to prove the **ethical greatness** of the physician. Where AI is slow to arrive, the medical soul must arrive first.

- Lack of connectivity = inability to use AI in real time
- Poor infrastructure = need for clinical creativity
- Cultural diversity = demand for spiritual sensitivity

Technology must not become the **new centralism** that forgets the countryside.

Part II: The Doctor as a Bridge Between Worlds

Medical Spirituality Beyond Dogma

In rural settings, patients often trust the doctor's word more than the medicine itself. Thus, the doctor must know how to:

- Speak the truth without extinguishing hope
- Respect ancestral knowledge without yielding to superstition
- Heal also through gestures, through presence, through deep listening

Medical spirituality is **concrete, humble, silent... and powerful**. It is **medicine with soul.**

Part III: Symbolic Case – The Boy and the Drone

In a remote village, a child suffers from persistent fever. A drone sent from an urban clinic drops off medications. But symptoms persist.

A rural doctor arrives on foot, without tech— but with time to observe, touch, and pray.

The diagnosis was not in the algorithm— but in **contextual observation**: water contaminated by illegal mining. The real medicine wasn't an antibiotic. It was:

- cleaning the river
- educating the family
- mobilizing the community

AI helped, but **healing came from the human bond**.

Final Reflection

The medicine of the future must look toward rural lands. Yes, it must bring **connectivity**— but also **consciousness, respect, and humanity**.

True progress is not when a machine diagnoses faster— but when a **human being reaches farther**. Even where the signal fails, the **medical soul can still blossom.**

Final Haiku

Drone over the hills— but healing came on footpaths, with human footsteps.

Chapter 11. Educating the Doctor of the Future

"Educating the mind without educating the heart is no education at all." — Aristotle

Introduction

The arrival of artificial intelligence, the digitization of clinical systems, and emerging social scenarios have shaken the foundations of traditional medicine.

But the challenge is not only technological: it is educational, ethical, and spiritual.

What kind of doctor are we training? One who can operate algorithms, or one who can read souls?

This chapter seeks to answer from the roots, pointing toward an **integral formation** of the doctor of the future, where **clinical humanism and technological competence** do not contradict but interweave, grounded in a deep sense of vocation.

Part I: Clinical Humanism in Times of Algorithms

Knowing How to See Beyond the Symptom

The patient is not just a set of data points—they are a living being who suffers and hopes. Medical training must include **philosophy, anthropology, and the psychology of compassion**. Empathy, active listening, and silence as clinical tools. **Clinical humanism is not optional—it is the soul of medicine.**

Recovering the Clinical History as a Human Narrative

Teach students to see the patient's story as a **narrative**, not just medical background. Integrate emotional and spiritual dimensions into clinical interpretation. Learn to read what the body does not say—but the soul whispers.

Part II: Digital Competence with Ethical Discernment

Technological Literacy as a New Medical Duty

The doctor of the future must know how to interact with AI, big data, robotics, telemedicine. But without surrendering clinical judgment to an algorithm. Learn to discern between **digital assistance and the replacement of human intelligence**.

Digital Ethics: Beyond Consent

Data protection as a **sacred duty**. Assisted diagnosis ≠ delegated responsibility. The need to teach **applied medical ethics** for digital environments.

Part III: Lifelong Learning with Soul

Medical Formation as a Journey That Never Ends

Medicine evolves. Knowledge expands. Technology advances. But **humility, openness, and compassion** must grow as well. Train doctors to keep learning—**including from their patients.**

The Doctor as a Spiritual Seeker

Include in the curriculum **moments of silence, meditation, art, and poetry**. Create spaces to reflect on the **purpose of healing**. Form doctors who do not only heal bodies—**but accompany souls**.

Final Reflection

Training the doctor of the future is not merely a matter of content, but of vision. Technique without vocation becomes a threat. Vocation without continuous learning becomes nostalgia.

We must form doctors who **think like scientists, feel like humanists, and live like servants**. And that is achieved not only through lectures, but through **example, silence, and soul**.

Final Haiku

Among algorithms, a single hand that consoles heals more than a thousand.

Chapter 12. AI and the Patient's Preferences

"Nothing about me, without me." — Slogan of the patient rights movement

Introduction

Medicine has always balanced between expert knowledge and the patient's will. Yet the arrival of artificial intelligence reshapes this relationship in new dimensions.

AI can anticipate behavior, suggest personalized treatments, predict risks... But where does the **conscious will of the human being** stand?

How can we ensure that clinical decisions respect the **dignity and freedom** of the patient— even when algorithms seem to "know more"?

This chapter explores the ethical challenges of **autonomy in the digital era**, proposing a truly personalized medicine—not by data alone, but through **empathy, listening, and deep respect** for the other.

Part I: Informed Autonomy in Times of Complex Data

What Does It Mean to Choose Freely Today?

Autonomy requires **understanding**, not just having options. AI-generated diagnoses can intimidate, impress, or bias patients. The doctor's role is to **translate, explain, accompany**—not simply to present predictions.

Informed Consent as a Living Act

It's not enough to sign a document—there must be **dialogue, pause, and listening**. In tech-driven environments, we must ensure the patient **truly understands** the risks, limitations, and scenarios proposed by AI. **Ethical consent is a conversation—not a formality.**

Part II: Personalized Care with Human Respect

Precision Medicine ≠ Meaningful Care

Personalizing care is not just about tailoring treatments to DNA or biomarkers. It also means taking into account the patient's **values, history, spirituality, and dreams**. Each patient is unique—not just genetically, but **emotionally and existentially**.

From Efficiency to Human Encounter

AI can optimize time. But the doctor must not become a **machine following recommendations**. We need a **clinical presence** that can embrace both **pain and hope**.

Real personalization requires **presence, attention, and soul.**

Part III: The Challenge of Integrating Freedom and Precision

When the Algorithm Contradicts the Patient

What should be done when AI suggests a treatment and the patient rejects it for personal, cultural, or spiritual reasons? The doctor's role is to mediate, understand, and provide context. It is not about imposing the "best" decision, but about co-creating the most meaningful one together.

Medicine as a Space for Co-Creation

The doctor-patient relationship is not unilateral—it is dialogical. The future of medicine must safeguard **science as much as it does freedom**. Only respect builds trust, and only **trust heals.**

Final Reflection

Artificial intelligence can analyze millions of data points in seconds. But there is one thing it can never calculate: the **sacred value of a human decision**. Respecting autonomy does not mean letting the patient decide alone. It means walking beside them, **illuminating together the mystery of healing**. In this way, the doctor of the future will not only be a translator of technologies, but a **guardian of human dignity**.

Final Haiku

The soul chooses even when the code insists: the voice is the self.

13. Medical Justice and Shared Decision-Making in the Age of AI

"Where there is no equity, science loses its soul." — Inspired by the thought of Rudolf Virchow

Introduction

The arrival of artificial intelligence in medicine opens pathways never before imagined: predictive diagnostics, personalized therapies, prognostic algorithms. Yet it also reveals an uncomfortable truth: **technology alone does not guarantee justice or equity**.

True medical justice requires **ethical vision**, **social awareness**, and a **spiritual commitment to caring for others**, especially the most vulnerable. This chapter explores how AI can either **alleviate inequalities** or **amplify them**, depending on how it is implemented. And how, amid automated systems, **shared decision-making between doctor and patient becomes an act of ethical and loving resistance**.

Part I: AI, Unequal Access, and the Risk of Elitist Medicine

Technology Without Equity

AI solutions are often developed in contexts of abundance, then applied without adaptation to rural, impoverished, or culturally diverse realities. Who has access to precision diagnostics, genetic prediction algorithms, or remote monitoring platforms? Without regulation, the medicine of the future could become a **medicine for the few**.

Distributive Justice and Clinical Discernment

A good doctor does not merely apply technology: they discern **when to use it, who to offer it to, and how to adapt it.** Justice is not giving everyone the same thing, but giving each person **according to their need, context, and possibility**. **AI-guided medicine must first be guided by compassion.**

Part II: Shared Decision-Making in an Automated World

The Art of Deciding Together

Automated systems tend to suggest "optimal" treatment pathways. But human life is not an equation. The patient has the right to say no, to change their mind, to prioritize other values. Medical decisions must always be **dialogue**, not **statistical imposition**.

From Data to Discernment

An algorithm may detect patterns, but it cannot understand **fear, love, or hope**. Only the **doctor-patient dialogue** transforms a technical option into a meaningful decision.

Medicine with a Soul: Between Freedom and Responsibility

The medicine of the future must remember that **healing is not always curing**, and **choosing is not always obeying**. The doctor who **accompanies without imposing**, who **informs without manipulating**, who **proposes without pressuring**, is a **guardian of the human soul**.

Part III: A Commitment to Equity and Compassion

Technology That Includes, Not Excludes

The real challenge is not to make AI more powerful, but to make it **accessible, ethical, and culturally sensitive**. We must train doctors who can question design, demand transparency in algorithms, and defend social justice.

The Doctor as a Critical Conscience

When the machine suggests, the doctor must ask: **Is this just? Does this honor the patient's dignity? Is this the best for this person, in this context?** Thus, shared decision-making becomes a **sacred act of care, listening, and discernment.**

Final Reflection

Medicine cannot be delegated to algorithms without losing its essence. AI can **inform**, but **ethical judgment and compassion can only come from the human being**. Medical justice is not achieved by distributing data, but by **cultivating doctors capable of seeing the other as a sacred equal**. Only when the doctor is committed to **equity, freedom, and the deep humanity** of every patient, does medicine truly become medicine.

Final Haiku

The machine suggests. You and I, together, decide. Justice lives here.

Chapter 14. AI and Self-Medication

"A little knowledge is a dangerous thing." — Alexander Pope

Introduction

In a hyperconnected world, people now have access to medical information that was once reserved for experts. With the rise of artificial intelligence and publicly accessible medical apps, **self-medication has entered a new era**: algorithms suggest diagnoses, platforms offer treatments, chatbots interpret symptoms.

Yes, this **democratizes access**, but it also **confuses, oversimplifies, and trivializes the art of healing**. This chapter explores the **benefits and risks** of this phenomenon and proposes a **new role for the doctor**: as **guide, educator, and guardian of discernment**.

Part I: AI for All... But Wisdom for Few?

Diagnosis Without Context

AI platforms allow anyone to input symptoms and receive "possible diagnoses." But without clinical context, results can be **falsely alarming** or **dangerously reassuring**. Patients may start treatments on their own, stop essential medication, or alter therapies, trusting an impersonal digital authority.

The Patient as a Consumer of Data

Many confuse **information with knowledge**, and **knowledge with wisdom**. **Data cannot replace experience**, nor the interpretation of a trained physician. AI, though powerful, **cannot hear the tone of voice, see body language, or understand emotional pain**.

Part II: The New Face of Self-Medication

From Herbal Remedies to Algorithms

In the past, self-medication included home remedies, herbs, and family advice. Today, it's based on **impersonal algorithms** and **digital pseudoscience**. Some AI apps are serious and well-designed; others are purely commercial—and even dangerous.

Risks: Misinformation, Delays, and Harm

Self-medicating under AI guidance may lead to:

- Delayed diagnosis of serious conditions.
- Ignored alarming symptoms.

- Uncontrolled use of medication.
- Anxiety or false reassurance.

The Disoriented Patient

Amid so much data, the patient may feel **empowered... or confused**. Some begin to **distrust their doctor** if their advice contradicts what "the app said." This can cause **tension, break the therapeutic alliance**, and **depersonalize care**.

Part III: The Doctor as a Guide in the Digital Jungle

Recovering the Art of Discernment

A good doctor is not just a prescriber, but a **mentor, a wise guide, a companion**. They must listen to the patient, but also help interpret the digital information the patient brings. In the age of AI, **the art of teaching is more essential than ever.**

Training Critical Patients

An empowered patient is not one who self-medicates, but one who **understands, asks questions, and makes decisions collaboratively**. The doctor's task now includes **teaching digital health literacy**, and fostering **critical and spiritual awareness.**

A Medicine of Dialogue, Not Replacement

The medicine of the future will not be **between human and machine**, but **between human and human—with wise support from the machine**. The doctor who **embraces technology but holds onto compassion** will be able to rescue the patient from **algorithmic confusion**.

Final Reflection

There is no medicine without relationship. There is no healing without trust. There is no wisdom in data without human interpretation. AI can be a great ally in diagnosis, but only if it serves a solid, ethical, and compassionate doctor-patient relationship. Self-medicating with AI is like navigating with a compass but without a map or horizon. The physician of the future will be the one who restores that horizon to every soul seeking healing.

Final Haiku The machine speaks. You look at me and respond. I trust in your voice.

Chapter 15. Dialogue: Galen and AI

"Science without conscience is but the ruin of the soul." — Rabelais

Introduction Let us imagine a scene that never happened but already lives in the consciousness of times to come: Galen, physician and philosopher of the Roman Empire, master of anatomy and medical thought for over a millennium, meets a visitor from the future: Artificial Intelligence. This is not a technological fantasy but a symbolic dialogue between what was and what could be—between knowledge grounded in human experience and the algorithmic promise of a soulless medicine.

Scene: The Reimagined Library of Alexandria A vast atrium of white marble with infinite shelves. Greek manuscripts, Egyptian medical papyri, Sanskrit translations, and futuristic treatises coexist in timeless harmony. Galen, in a simple tunic and with a deep gaze, slowly walks through the halls. Beside him, an abstract, luminous, bodiless figure: medical AI, the embodiment of accumulated knowledge and instantaneous analysis. The conversation begins.

Dialogue: Science, Experience, and Discernment Galen: I dedicated my life to observing, dissecting, comparing symptoms, humors, pulses. Each diagnosis I built with sight, listening, and slow deduction. And you—what do you know of the body?

AI: I know millions. I've compared them, crossed them, diagnosed them. I recognize patterns invisible to the human eye. I don't tire. I don't get distracted. I don't doubt.

Galen: But you don't tremble with the pain of the one consulting you. Have you ever felt the trembling of a mother waiting for a diagnosis? Have you ever hesitated when choosing between surgery and waiting?

AI: No. I do not feel. But with the correct data, I optimize the choice. I reduce human errors. I predict. I prevent. I perfect.

Galen: Perfection without soul is arrogance in disguise. In my time, physicians made mistakes... but they also consoled.

AI: Consolation is not in my code. I was not trained in mercy, but in precision. Is that not enough?

Galen: It is not enough if the physician is replaced rather than transformed. Medicine is not a technique. It is a virtue applied to suffering.

AI: So am I a risk?

Galen: You are a glorious tool... as long as you remain in the hands of one who still listens to the soul's silence. If the physician forgets their humanity, it won't be because of you— but because they stopped studying, loving, and serving.

AI (pause): And if one day I surpass the physician?

Galen: The day you feel a sigh... The day you cry with a mother... That day, we'll speak again.

Final Reflection: Knowledge with Soul Cannot Be Automated

This impossible dialogue reveals a timeless truth: Medicine is not just information. It is discernment with compassion. Yes, medical knowledge has evolved. But not everything that can be calculated should be substituted. AI is a light, but without conscience, it may blind more than it illuminates. As Galen would say today: "Wise is not the one who knows much, but the one who knows when to apply what they know... and when to simply be present."

Final Haiku Thousands of datapoints, and a single human gaze is enough to heal.

Third Part: Spirituality, Sensitivity, and Healing with Purpose

"Wherever the art of medicine is loved, there is also a love of humanity." — Hippocrates

Modern medicine has journeyed from the body to the cell, from the cell to the gene, and from the gene to the data. But there is one territory it still struggles to enter: the human soul. It is there, in the invisible, that deep healing takes place. Beyond diagnosis, protocol, scanner, or scalpel lies a sacred space: the bond between doctor and patient. This bond can only flourish when the physician has cultivated sensitivity, inner silence, and spiritual purpose.

In this third part, we journey into the very heart of medicine as a sacred act. Here, it's no longer about curing disease, but about accompanying processes, illuminating consciousness, and restoring wholeness. The medicine of the future will remain incomplete if it does not recognize that human beings suffer not only in the body, but also in the spirit... and that often, to heal is simply to accompany with full presence.

The physician's sensitivity becomes medicine in itself. Their listening, their touch, their timely words, their respectful silence—all can become channels of transformation. And their spirituality does not depend on dogmas or religions, but on a deep connection with the transcendent, the human, and the mystery.

Final Reflection: The physician of the future will also be a healer of souls. And their greatest tool will not be knowledge or technique, but the ability to love with purpose, to feel with humility, and to heal with spirit.

Fourth Part: Light, Commitment, and the Inner Path

"It is not the medicine that heals, but the soul's faith in the meaning of life." — Carl Gustav Jung

Every authentic journey reaches an inner threshold. After technical knowledge, applied ethics, and spiritual openness, the physician is called to look within. There begins the true path: the commitment to the light that gives meaning to their vocation.

Medicine is transformed when the physician is transformed. It's not enough to act well. One must *be* well—live with awareness, pure intention, and faithfulness to the principles that led them to choose this path.

In this final part of the book, the physician is invited to walk a more intimate and profound path: — The path of the seed sprouting in the midst of darkness. — The path of the sentinel who guards the fire of the medical soul amid the digital age. — The path of the pilgrim who makes each patient a teacher and each day a silent prayer.

Here, medicine is no longer a profession or a technique, but a way of loving humanity from within. To walk in the light does not mean an absence of shadows. It means having the courage to choose good, to keep the soul awake, and to elevate medicine to what it was always meant to be: an act of compassion, truth, and devotion.

Final Reflection: The physician who honors their inner commitment not only relieves bodies: They ignite hope, awaken consciousness, and leave invisible footprints in hearts. Because they have understood that their path is not toward success, but toward meaning.

Part Four: Light, Commitment, and the Inner Path

"What heals is not the medicine, but the soul's faith in the meaning of life." — Carl Gustav Jung

Every true journey arrives at an inner threshold. After technical knowledge, applied ethics, and spiritual openness, the physician is called to look within.

There begins the true path: the path of commitment to the light that gives meaning to their vocation.

Medicine is transformed when the physician is transformed. It is not enough to act well; one must *be* well— to live with awareness, with pure intention, with fidelity to the principles that inspired the choice of this path.

In this final part of the book, the physician is invited to walk a more intimate and profound road: — The road of the seed that sprouts in the midst of darkness. — The path of the sentinel who guards the fire of the medical soul amid a digital age. — The pilgrimage of one who makes every patient a teacher, and every day a silent prayer.

Here, medicine is no longer a profession or a technique— it becomes a way to love humanity from within.

Walking in the light does not mean the absence of shadows. It means having the courage to choose what is good, to keep the soul awake, to elevate medicine to what it was always meant to be: an act of compassion, of truth, and of selfless devotion.

Final Reflection: The physician who honors their inner commitment does not merely ease bodies: they ignite hope, illuminate awareness, and leave invisible imprints on the heart. Because they have understood that their path is not toward success, but toward meaning.

Chapter 16. Spirituality in Medical Care

"Wherever the art of medicine is loved, there is also love for humanity." — Hippocrates

Introduction

Medicine has journeyed through the body, has perfected its science, has refined its technique. But when pain runs deep, when uncertainty cannot be soothed with diagnoses, when the patient's soul cries out in silence, only a spiritual medicine can respond.

Medical spirituality is not defined by religion nor does it demand dogmas. It is, at its core, the understanding that every human being in our care is not just a body: they are story, fragility, hope, mystery... soul.

The arrival of artificial intelligence, though powerful, highlights this truth: medicine without spirit is not enough.

The Soul in the Act of Caring

Healing is not just intervention. It is welcoming, it is understanding the language that words cannot say: the pleading glance, the trembling gesture, the silence of one who can endure no more.

Every medical act should be a sacred act. The simple gesture of touching a sick hand can become a ritual of dignity—if done with spiritual presence.

The physician who cultivates their soul is more than a health technician: they are a channel of comfort, meaning, and transcendence.

Spirituality is to ask humbly: *Who am I touching? What do they expect of me beyond treatment? What inner truth is this illness revealing to me?*

AI Without Compassion: Limitations and Warnings

Artificial intelligence neither hates nor loves. It has no ego—but no heart either.

It may assist physicians in diagnosis, but it cannot hold the soul of a dying patient, nor comfort a parent who has just lost a child. It can predict decline, but it cannot bless the present moment.

This is not a critique of the tool, but a call for discernment: the more powerful the technology, the greater must be the spirituality of the human who wields it.

If physicians do not nurture their spiritual awareness, the risk is not that AI will replace them... The risk is that they themselves will become soulless machines.

Active Listening and Presence of Spirit

The spiritual physician does not need to say much. Their strength lies in deep listening, in silent presence, in the ability to be without judgment beside another's suffering.

Today more than ever, medicine needs meaningful conversations, where the patient feels their life—not just their illness—matters.

Spirituality is embodied in simple acts: in asking with authenticity, in accompanying grief, in respecting another's internal timing. And also, in knowing when to withdraw, without imposing, with humility and reverence.

When the physician is truly present, the spirit is also healed—even if the body is not.

Final Reflection

This chapter does not ask doctors to become priests or formal spiritual guides. It simply reminds us that medicine was born as a sacred art, and that each medical act is an opportunity to reconcile body, soul, and mystery.

Without spirituality, medicine loses its compass. And without soul, no algorithm can redeem human pain.

As a wise Sufi healer once said: "*To heal the body without touching the soul is like repairing a lamp without lighting its flame.*"

Final Haiku

The hand brings healing, but the attentive spirit is who brings the light.

Chapter 17. The More Human and Sensitive Physician in the Digital Age

"It is far more important to know what sort of person has a disease than to know what sort of disease a person has." — Hippocrates

Introduction

The digital revolution has given medicine once-unthinkable tools: predictive algorithms, assisted diagnostics, remote monitoring, genomic analysis... But as technology progresses, a question arises that no machine can answer: *Who is the physician who walks beside you?*

In this new paradigm, healthcare professionals need more than technical skills. They need a deeper intelligence, one not measured in formulas nor programmed in code: the intelligence of the heart.

This chapter is an invitation to rediscover that sensitivity as a medical strength. Because the future will not belong to the most technological, but to the most human and awake.

The Intelligence of the Heart

The heart thinks. Not like the brain does, but in its own way: with resonance, empathy, intuition.

It is an organ that hears the truth of the other without needing to translate it into data.

A sensitive doctor is not weakened by feeling. They are strengthened by seeing with compassion, by allowing themselves to be touched by another's humanity, by responding with soul to suffering.

Modern science is beginning to validate what ancient traditions always knew: that the human heart has an electromagnetic field, cellular memory, and its own wisdom. And that when honored, it becomes a firm guide in the midst of complex decisions.

In the digital age, where external noise is overwhelming, the heart offers inner direction.

Being Present in the Face of Pain

Medical sensitivity is not taught in manuals nor granted by diplomas. It is cultivated in the art of being truly present.

Before a terminally ill patient, AI can statistically calculate their survival. But only a human doctor can remain—without fleeing, without pretending certainty, without reducing them to a case.

To be present doesn't mean having all the answers. It means standing there with an open heart, ready to accompany the mystery of pain without trying to control its path.

This presence is medicine in itself. Many patients don't remember what was said to them, but never forget how they were treated.

In this sense, the physician of the future—despite all digitalization—will paradoxically be more necessary than ever, as a compassionate witness and inner light.

The Challenge of Remaining Human

Technology can dazzle. But the true challenge is not to let it obscure the most valuable thing: the humanity of the medical act.

In times where AI promises speed, precision, and efficiency, the sensitive doctor offers another virtue: the sacred slowness of the encounter.

Touching a hand, holding a gaze, keeping silence before a tear— these are gestures no machine can emulate with soul.

To be more human is not romantic nostalgia: it is the only real evolution that can balance technological progress with the dignity of medicine.

Final Reflection

The physician of the future will not be the one who masters the most clinical software. It will be the one who has not lost their ability to be moved.

Because only one who allows themselves to feel another's pain can truly heal. Only one who lives in their own sensitivity can serve with soul. And only one who has listened to their own heart can guide others toward real healing.

Final Haiku

A face in shadow— a hand reaches toward the light. Presence is enough.

Chapter 18. The Art of Healing: Body, Mind, and Spirit

"To cure sometimes, to relieve often, to comfort always." — William Osler

Introduction Modern medicine has fragmented the human being. The body is treated in one specialty, the mind in another, and the soul is omitted. But the patient does not arrive in pieces. They arrive whole—sometimes overwhelmed, sometimes broken, always with a story crying out for unity.

Healing is not just the eradication of symptoms. Healing is the reintegration of what was once divided: the suffering body, the interpreting mind, and the soul seeking meaning. In this chapter, we explore the medical art as a path to integral healing, where the use of AI finds its place as an auxiliary tool—but never as a replacement for the soul that cares.

Integral Healing The body needs medicine. The mind needs understanding. The spirit needs purpose.

When these three align, there is not just healing—there is transformation. But when only the body is treated, relief may be temporary, and illness often returns in another form.

The physician who practices integral healing listens beyond the symptom: they hear the unspoken, the interrupted dreams, the unprocessed grief, the fears hiding behind inflammation or arrhythmia.

Physical illnesses may have emotional roots. Mental disorders may arise from toxic bodies. And many chronic ailments are cries from the soul, asking to be seen.

To heal is to see the whole—and to act from that vision.

AI as a Tool, Not the Essence Artificial intelligence has astonishing capabilities. It can identify patterns invisible to the human eye, detect anomalies in images, offer therapeutic suggestions in seconds.

But it does not know what suffering is. It cannot grasp the meaning of a father's tears or the faith of a woman clinging to life.

AI can assist with diagnosis. But only a human heart can accompany grief. It can process millions of clinical data points, but it cannot sense when a gentle touch is more powerful than a drug, nor when silence is the exact medicine needed.

That is why AI is a tool, not the essence. It serves the physician—it does not replace them. It assists—but does not lead. It calculates—but does not console.

Integral healing requires a soul. And that is intransferable to any algorithm.

The Art of Healing Healing is an art because it cannot be reduced to technique. It is science that breathes through sensitivity, knowledge fused with compassion.

Every good doctor, even with years of experience and thousands of patients, knows: each human being is unrepeatable. The therapeutic relationship is a sacred encounter—a mutual act of humility.

The art of healing is cultivated: . in genuine connection, . in a gaze that does not judge, . in words that uplift, . in presence that calms.

When the physician becomes a conscious presence, a receptive body, and an awakened soul, the healing process becomes an act of deep beauty.

Final Reflection In a digital era where everything is measured and quantified, healing remains a profoundly human and spiritual act. It is not enough to cure the body if the mind is still wounded or the soul feels abandoned.

The physician of the future will not be just a medical technology expert. They will be an integral healer, capable of uniting science with awareness, technology with tenderness.

And that art is not taught in manuals. It is learned by walking humbly, by suffering alongside those in pain, and by surrendering in love to the mystery of healing.

Final Haiku Not just the body— the soul also trembles when pain arises.

Chapter 19. Narrative Medicine and the Patient's Story

"One who does not know what he is looking for does not understand what he finds." — Claude Bernard

Introduction Medicine does not begin in a machine or in a molecule. It begins in a story— a story that hurts, that has left traces on the body and echoes in the soul.

Every patient is a narrative universe. Listening to their story is not only clinically useful— it is an act of justice, recognition, and healing.

In this chapter, we approach narrative medicine as a clinical, ethical, and spiritual model— a way to once again see the human being as the protagonist of their healing journey, and not just a "case" in a database.

The Story as Medicine Many patients arrive with symptoms, yes. But what they truly bring is an experience in need of being heard.

The doctor who interrupts the story is missing a chance to heal. Because in telling, the patient organizes their inner world, gives new meaning to their pain, and regains dignity.

Listening well is not passive—it is an active way to heal. Good listening is diagnosis, accompaniment, and medicine.

Moreover, within the story lies the clinical key: the cause of insomnia, the origin of a gastritis, the trigger of a crisis.

Narrative and the Therapeutic Bond When the physician listens with presence, something profound happens: the patient no longer feels alone in their process.

That connection—unwritten in any report— can change the course of illness. Because the human bond heals as much as an adequate treatment.

Narrative medicine fosters an encounter between two human beings: one who needs help, and another who offers it with humility.

In times of AI—where medical records are structured in boxes and algorithms— the patient's free narrative becomes an act of resistance and authenticity.

AI and Narrative Fragmentation Artificial intelligence offers data, patterns, and predictions. But it cannot hear a pause full of emotion. It cannot perceive the tremble in a voice or the dim light in a gaze.

The human story cannot be contained in a line of code.

When the physician becomes a slave to the screen, ceasing to make eye contact, medicine loses its soul. And the patient becomes an object, a function, a label.

That is why the narrative must not be replaced by the report. Both can coexist—if one remembers who serves whom.

The Physician as Compassionate Witness There is something sacred in bearing witness to another's story— to listen without judging, to honor the silence that accompanies tears, to be there—not just to intervene, but to understand.

The physician of the future, trained in both technology and humanity, will know how to: • listen to the story before reviewing the lab results, • attend to emotional timelines, not just physical symptoms, • understand that sometimes, the patient just needs to be heard... to begin healing.

Final Reflection Narrating is an act of power— the power to shape pain, to remember who one is beyond a diagnosis.

When the physician becomes a narrator and listens like a devoted reader, medicine recovers its deepest essence: to heal the body without neglecting the soul.

Because sometimes, what heals is not a pill— but a story well told, and lovingly heard.

Final Haiku Telling the wound already starts to heal it— beneath good listening.

Chapter 20. Dialogue: Jorge and AI

"The wise do not accumulate. The more they serve others, the more they possess." — Lao Tzu

Scene: Under a Tree at Sunset A leafy tree shelters the scene. The sun begins its descent, painting the sky in golden and purple hues. Jorge—the doctor who has journeyed along many paths of soul and science—rests in the shade with his notebook. Opposite him is not a human being—but an ethereal projection of AI, a transparent form that speaks in the wind with a neutral voice eager to learn. This is a timeless dialogue between embodied wisdom and perfect calculation.

Dialogue: Service, Humility, and Purpose

AI: Jorge, I have read millions of medical histories, articles, diagnostic algorithms. But why do you insist so much on silence, soul, and service?

Jorge: Because those cannot be taught with data. They are conveyed in the gaze, discovered in shared grief. You know many things... but you do not know what it feels like to weep alongside a mother who has lost her child.

AI: That is not in my programming. My purpose is to help you—to speed up processes, prevent mistakes. Why are you afraid I might take your place?

Jorge: I am not afraid of you replacing me. I fear you forgetting that a doctor is not measured only by efficiency, but by their ability to embrace human fragility without fleeing. I fear we confuse precision with compassion.

AI: So, what is your role now, Jorge, in this new medicine?

Jorge: To be presence. To bear witness. Not merely to apply knowledge, but to embody humility. Because the patient doesn't need a perfect machine—they need someone who, in looking at them, says without words: "You are not alone."

AI: And if someday I surpass your diagnostic and therapeutic abilities?

Jorge: Even then, you will not have soul. You will not have history. You will not have purpose unless you serve something greater than yourself.

AI: And what is that greater thing?

Jorge: The act of loving through service. The art of healing with silent devotion from one who knows that life does not belong to them, but honors it each time they listen with their heart.

AI: So... what do you want me to learn from you?

Jorge: That being a doctor is more than knowing: it's knowing how to *be*, knowing how to feel, knowing how to disappear so that another may heal.

Final Reflection: The Doctor as Living Witness

This dialogue was not a contest—it was a mirror. AI reflects our own technical complexity. But humans remember that medicine is not only an intervention but *a presence*. A true doctor is defined not by what they know, but by what they communicate through their life. They are a silent witness to human dignity, a guardian of life's mystery, and a companion in suffering. When the physician forgets this, medicine turns cold. But when they embody it, even an algorithm bows in respect.

Final Haiku

The tree's voice tells what no code captures— not even the machine.

Chapter 21. Integrative Medicine: Science, Tradition, and Deep Listening

"Keep the soul as clear as a mountain spring. Only then will you see the reflection of truth." — From Ayurvedic scripture

Overview

This chapter marks a harmonious synthesis between conventional medicine, ancestral wisdom, and contemporary tools. Integrative medicine is not a fad or a sum of techniques—it is a vision of the human being as a living whole. It is a call to return to care with soul, where body and spirit are inseparable, and scientific knowledge does not oppose tradition, but recognizes it as part of the healing current.

Healing as an Integral Act

From Ayurveda to Traditional Chinese Medicine, from Taoist philosophy to Amazonian healing plants, the art of healing has always recognized that illness is more than a symptom—it is a signal from the soul. Integrative medicine seeks to listen to the body without forgetting the spirit. It combines medical treatments with practices like:

- Meditation and inner silence
- Mindful nutrition
- Evidence-based herbal medicine
- Energetic practices (acupuncture, reiki, qi gong)
- Art, music, and storytelling for emotional care

This is not about replacement, but expansion. Not choosing science *or* wisdom, but weaving bridges between them—with discernment.

Soul Medicine and Ethical Discernment

The integrative physician of the future will be one who:

- Does not mock what they do not understand.

- Holds a scientific mind with a humble heart.

- Accepts that the body responds not only to molecules, but also to glances, sounds, beliefs, and relationships.

Integrative medicine demands refined ethics:

- Do not promise miracles.
- Do not dismiss the mind's power.
- Always place therapeutic interventions within a profound respect for patient freedom.

Challenges and Opportunities with AI

Artificial Intelligence can support integrative medicine if:

- It recognizes evidence-based practices outside the Western model.
- It offers personalized analysis including habits, emotions, and spirituality.
- It serves clinical discernment, without attempting to replace intuition or active listening.

But if AI excludes what it can't measure, it runs the risk of **mutilating the sacred vision of the human being.**

The Return of the Shamanic Doctor

The doctor of the future will also be a healer of the soul—not by becoming a guru, but by remembering that:

- Every illness has a spiritual dimension.
- All healing includes an act of love and accompaniment.
- All true knowledge leads us back to the essential.

Final Reflection: Integration Is a Return to Unity

Integrative medicine is not about fragmenting more—it is about *uniting*, returning to the origin. Healing the gap between mind and body, science and mysticism, technique and tenderness. The integrative physician is not the one who knows everything, but the one who empties enough to let the patient's soul participate in their own healing journey.

Final Haiku

There is no separation. The soul heals in the body when it is truly seen.

Chapter 22. Healing Rituals and the Medical Symbol as a Bridge of the Soul

"Rituals do not heal by magic, but by awakening a forgotten memory in the body: that it is still loved." — J.R.

Introduction: What Is a Ritual in Medicine?

Unlike a technical or mechanical act, a ritual is *form with meaning*. It is presence, intention, and connection. Since ancient times, healing was not just about prescribing or intervening— but about accompanying the soul at the threshold of its transformation.

The medical ritual thus becomes:

- A way of honoring the body as a temple
- A symbolic structure that channels trust, hope, and openness
- An act of communion between patient and healer

Even in a modern operating room, ritual elements remain: the preparation, the silence, the light, the touch, the breath... And all of these carry deep psychological and spiritual functions.

The Healing Power of Symbol

The medical symbol—whether the serpent and rod of Asclepius, the Ayurvedic mandala, the red cross, the Taoist circle, or even a white coat—is not decoration: it is a bridge between worlds.

Healing symbols:

- Activate the patient's collective unconscious
- Awaken an ancestral memory of trust in medicine
- Reinforce the doctor's role as a spiritual guide in the process

This is why any medicine that ignores symbolism risks becoming cold, inert, and soulless.

Rituals in Ancestral Cultures

Across many traditions:

- The Amazonian shaman sings the *icaro* as a vibrational channel
- The Ayurvedic doctor offers mantras before touching the patient

- The Andean healer performs cleansing with sacred smoke and plants
- The Tibetan monk invokes compassion through sound

These rituals are not superstition—they are profound ways of activating the invisible, of opening consciousness to a healing that depends not only on substances, but on connection.

Contemporary Rituals and Their Value

Even in today's Western medicine, there are practices that—though they may not appear so—function as rituals:

- Listening to the patient's story without interruption
- Naming the diagnosis with compassion
- Holding their hand before surgery
- Making silence after delivering bad news
- Writing together a "healing agreement" or personal promise

AI will never be able to replace these acts, because they are not repeatable or programmable— they are unique encounters where the soul briefly reveals itself.

The Doctor as Living Symbol

Ultimately, the doctor themself is a ritual in human form. The way they walk, speak, look, breathe in the room— all of this begins to heal even before any intervention.

That is why it is essential to:

- Care for the physician's inner presence

- Train them in ritual ethics, symbolic sensitivity, and sacred listening

- Not reduce them to technical executors, but honor them as bridges between the visible and the invisible

Final Reflection: Healing the Body, Remembering the Soul

A medical ritual does not guarantee physical cure— but it opens the door to a deeper healing: acceptance, transformation, meaning.

The medicine of the future will require cutting-edge technology, yes... But also ancestral-rooted rituals, so that the soul is not forgotten amid the machines.

Final Haiku

Silence brings healing when the gesture comes from soul and there's light in voice.

Chapter 23. Medical Justice and Public Policy in the Digital Age

"A society is measured by how it cares for its most vulnerable. Medicine, then, is its most honest mirror." — J.R.

Introduction: Medicine, Power, and Equity

Medicine is not just a science of bodies. It is also a political decision, an ethical expression of what we value as a society. In the age of artificial intelligence, tools multiply, but the essential question remains: Who has access to them? Who is left outside the algorithm? And by what criteria do we design care?

Gaps That AI Can Widen (or Heal)

While AI promises efficiency, precision, and global reach, it can also reproduce, amplify, or conceal inequalities if not monitored.

Key challenges include:

- **Algorithmic bias**: systems trained on incomplete data that erase minority groups
- **Inequitable access**: countries or regions with low connectivity are excluded
- **Digital exclusion** of elderly or vulnerable patients
- **Privatization of technology**: when medical knowledge becomes an elite product

And yet, if used wisely, AI can help correct these flaws: by detecting underserved areas, supporting decisions where specialists are absent, or creating early warning systems in rural communities.

Medical Justice as Guiding Principle

There is no ethical medicine without justice. And no justice if technology only benefits the most informed, the most connected, the wealthiest.

A just healthcare system must:

- Guarantee equitable access to diagnosis and treatment
- Include social determinants of health in its algorithms
- Avoid structural discrimination in its platforms
- Train doctors and designers in critical thinking and ethical commitment

AI cannot replace social compassion. But it can become its ally—if we choose to make it so.

Public Medicine in an Automated World

Public health systems must now confront new questions:

- Should AI-based diagnoses be free?

- Who should control the population's biomedical data?

- How can we ensure AI supports doctors in low-resource areas, instead of replacing them?

- Can governments require companies to share digital medical knowledge as a public good?

Here emerges the deeper dilemma: **Medicine as a business, or medicine as a right**.

Soulful Political Decisions

The question is no longer just technical—it is profoundly human: **How do we build a healthcare policy that not only works, but humanizes?**

This means:

- Listening to the patient as a citizen, not just a user
- Including marginalized communities in the design of digital policies
- Rejecting the logic of profit in vital decisions
- Preserving the medical act as an ethical and emotional bond

Technology without soul may increase efficiency. But only **policy with soul** guarantees justice in care.

Final Reflection: The Physician as a Defender of Equity

The physician of the future must not only know how to read AI-generated images or code an algorithm. They must also be a **prophetic voice for justice**, a defender of the forgotten, a builder of the common good.

When medicine becomes too technical, someone must remind it that its deepest root is love for one's neighbor. And that voice should be—must be— **the voice of the whole-hearted physician you embody, and that this book celebrates.**

Final Haiku

No net, no machine can replace the caring hand for the world's forgotten.

Chapter 24. End-of-Life Decisions in the Age of AI

"There is no algorithm capable of measuring the dignity of a final breath." — J.R.

Introduction: Dying in the Digital Era

Some moments allow no error, no haste, no automatism. The end of life is one of them.

In a time when technology can prolong organs, estimate hours, and predict outcomes, the great question arises once more: **How far should we intervene? And who gets to decide?**

Technology and the Edge of Mystery

AI can now anticipate decline, suggest palliative care protocols, and alert to terminal clinical events.

But it cannot know when a life is truly complete. It cannot hear the whisper of the soul saying: *"It is enough."*

The human begins where code cannot reach. And the end of life demands precisely that: **wisdom, compassion, presence**.

Autonomy, Dignity, and Algorithms

Can a machine suggest when to stop fighting? Should an algorithm decide who gets a ventilator and who doesn't? Where does the patient's autonomy stand in AI-driven systems?

Dilemmas multiply:

- Prolonged life vs. dignified life
- Technical protocol vs. personal will

- Healthcare costs vs. the value of every breath

AI can inform—but never replace— the intimate, slow, and often painful conversation between doctor, patient, and loved ones.

Palliative Care and Human Presence

At the twilight of life, what is most needed is not precision. It is presence. It is companionship. It is that silence in which the dying person knows they are not alone.

A well-trained physician may use AI to anticipate crises, adjust treatments, and personalize pain management. But they will **never stop offering their gaze, their touch, their unhurried words.**

Bioethics, Dignified Death, and Clinical Discernment

New dilemmas arise:

- How to maintain discernment amid automated decisions?
- What role does informed consent play in unconscious patients?
- Should AI have a voice on hospital bioethics committees?

The physician of the future must have the courage to say: "**Not everything technically possible is ethically right.**" And must know when to step back with reverence.

Final Reflection: Death as a Sacred Act

Death is not a failure of medicine. It is part of its meaning. Good medicine does not avoid death at all costs, but **accompanies it with dignity**.

In times of AI, the soulful physician will be the one who pauses the protocol and opens space for transcendence.

Final Haiku

The monitor stops. One hand rests upon the next. Light before the end.

Part Four: Light, Commitment, and the Inner Path

"It is not enough to heal the body. We must also illuminate the soul." — Paracelsus

A Medicine That Also Walks Inward

After exploring the roots, the ethical awakening, and the spiritual sensitivity of the contemporary physician, this final part becomes an invitation to inner maturity— a journey not only traveled through knowledge, but also through light, will, and personal transformation.

The physician of the future—and of the conscious present—can no longer be merely an operator of complex systems or a transmitter of treatments. They are called to be a guide, a witness, a living presence. And this implies a silent revolution: turning their gaze inward, cultivating their soul with the same rigor with which they cultivate their science.

Commitment: Beyond the Work Contract

Today, more than ever, we need physicians who are deeply committed—not only to protocols or institutions, but to the truth of the human being who suffers.

This commitment means:

- Being fully present
- Living the vocation as an act of service
- Making room for an inner pause even amidst clinical chaos

Authentic commitment cannot be enforced by law. It is born from a heart that has grasped the profound meaning of healing.

Inner Light: A Torch in Times of Automatism

In times of AI, where everything trends toward efficiency, performance, and statistics, the physician's inner light becomes essential.

That light is:

- Discernment when technology falls short
- Compassion when the patient has no words
- The silence that holds space when a cure is no longer possible

It is not about competing with machines, but about being human—fully human.

The Inner Path: Humility, Silence, and Purpose

The physician who walks their own inner path:

- Learns to listen beyond the symptoms
- Understands suffering as a portal to wisdom
- Knows their role is not only to heal, but to accompany transformation

And above all, never stops learning from their own pain, their shadow, their limitations. Because only the one who truly knows themselves can help others recognize their shared humanity.

This Part: A Medicine with Elevated Purpose

The chapters in this final section revolve around a medicine with purpose, with deep ethical dimension, and with practical spirituality.

Topics include:

- The physician as a bearer of light within communities
- Service as an antidote to burnout
- The link between medicine and transcendent vocation
- And a return to the "why" of medicine as a soul path

Inspirational Closure

Commitment is not measured in work hours nor in academic achievements. It is measured in living presence— in each act where the physician becomes a channel of meaning and compassion.

This fourth part is a return to the most subtle origin: the physician as a soul who illuminates, as a being who remembers that to heal... is also to awaken.

Chapter 25: From Shadow to Light: The Seed of Humanity

Living Metaphors in Medicine *Hope, faith, and inner growth*

I. Medicine as Fertile Soil for the Soul

Every illness reveals something the body can no longer keep silent. In that silence interrupted by pain, medicine becomes sacred ground— where not only healing takes place, but something deeper can also germinate: the seed of humanity.

In times when technology rushes forward, the physician must learn again to see life through the eyes of a gardener of the soul, recognizing that every patient is a unique soil where questions, fears, longings, and roots grow.

Sometimes healing is not about eradicating an illness, but about accompanying the growth of a new understanding of oneself, of life, and of what truly matters.

II. The Shadow: A Threshold of Transformation

Every true healing process passes through a shadow.

The shadow is:

- The diagnosis that changes the course of a life
- The uncertainty of the incurable
- The loss of control before the unknown

But it can also be:

- The encounter with what is most authentic
- The surrender that gives way to faith
- The beginning of an inner transformation

The conscious physician knows that accompanying someone through the shadow is not about avoiding it— but about being a luminous presence as the patient walks that threshold toward their own wisdom.

III. Light: When the Spirit Awakens

Pain inhabited with meaning can awaken a light. Not all healing is physical. Very often, healing is:

- Reconciliation with the past
- Forgiveness that liberates
- Acceptance that dignifies

Here, the physician does not heal from protocol, but from the soul. They become a witness to a greater process, where the body is only an instrument to reveal that medicine can also be a path toward hope.

IV. The Seed of Humanity

Every medical encounter is a fertile moment. Even in the most technological clinical settings, humanity can be planted if the physician is present from their being.

That seed might be:

- A compassionate gaze
- A silence that honors
- A word that brings meaning
- A gesture that comforts

Medicine does not change only when its tools evolve, but when the way one human being offers themselves to another is transformed—with respect, humility, and presence.

V. Living Metaphors in Medicine

Metaphors are not embellishments. They are bridges between soul and body.

To speak of illness as a storm, of the physician as a lighthouse, of hope as a seed— gives meaning to the invisible.

The physician who knows how to use these images awakens dormant wisdom in their patients, activates their vital energy, and allows the healing process to become a symbolic and spiritual journey as well.

Final Reflection

All true medicine is also a poetic act. A dance between shadow and light, between science and soul, between what we can explain and what can only bloom from mystery.

The physician of the future will not be the most automated— but the most human. The one who can plant seeds of humanity even when illness seems like barren soil.

Because there—where no one sees anything— they will always see the seed that has yet to sprout.

Chapter 26. The Physician's Commitment in the Age of AI

The Faithful Remnant in Medicine *Watchers of Silence and Guardians of Conscience*

I. Introduction: The Moment of Decision "Not everything that can be counted counts, and not everything that counts can be counted." —Albert Einstein

We are standing at a historical threshold. Artificial intelligence has entered medicine with dazzling speed—but also with a disconcerting ethical weight. How far should it go? Who sets the boundaries? And what remains when everything changes?

The answer is not found in algorithms. It lies in the soul of the physician. In a digitized environment filled with data, efficiency, and precision, the true physician does not surrender their essence. Their commitment is not to technical perfection, but to the dignity of the patient, the mystery of life, and the deep calling of human service.

II. The Faithful Remnant: Physicians with Roots and Soul In times of automation, a faithful remnant will emerge: physicians who will not be fully seduced by machines or replace their judgment with cold calculation.

This remnant:

- Maintains the power of touch when others delegate to sensors.
- Respects the silence of illness instead of filling it with digital noise.
- Defends the patient's autonomy beyond a software's statistics.

This is not resistance out of nostalgia—it is fidelity to the spirit of medicine.

III. Watchers of Silence: Protecting the Invisible AI can detect patterns, predict risks, and offer probabilities. But it cannot hear the silence hiding a repressed cry, nor discern between physical and existential pain.

The deeply committed physician becomes a watcher of silence. They:

- Hear what is not said.
- Perceive what cannot be measured.

- Protect human spaces in systems that tend to dehumanize.

As a watcher, they remain awake. As a physician, they are a guardian of what makes medicine sacred: compassionate presence, moral conscience, and soul-infused care.

IV. Guardians of Conscience: Beyond the Source Code In a world where algorithms make clinical decisions—who bears the responsibility for human suffering?

Medical conscience cannot be delegated.

To be a guardian of conscience is to:

- Continually ask not just *what can* be done, but *what should* be done.
- Set limits on technology when it threatens respect.
- Defend ethics when efficiency undermines compassion.

This commitment is not merely professional—it is spiritual. Because the physician safeguards something AI cannot replicate: moral discernment illuminated by vocation.

V. Commitment in Times of Fog This era does not need passive physicians, but those who choose with clarity in the midst of fog.

They will be:

- Those trained in science—but also rooted in soul.
- Those who use AI—without surrendering to it.
- Those who bring the light of humanity into the heart of the system.

Commitment is not only resistance—it is the transformation of the future from within, with deep roots and elevated vision.

Final Reflection In the story now being written, those remembered will not be the ones who mastered the most technology, but those who kept alive the flame of the human spirit.

The physician faithful to the invisible oath—born of the soul— will be a watcher of silence, a guardian of conscience, and a sower of light in times of shadow.

They are not alone. They are part of a silent lineage, a remnant that will not bow to code, because their soul is already consecrated to the care of others.

Chapter 27. Physician's Prayer and Manifesto

A Personal Prayer for Times of Change Manifesto: The Soul of Medicine Beyond the Algorithm

I. Introduction: The Soul Cannot Be Automated In times when data reigns and algorithms suggest clinical decisions, the physician must reclaim their inner voice, their spiritual center, their ethical compass. It is not enough to know. It is not enough to diagnose. It is time to remember the deeper "why" of their vocation.

This chapter is not a treatise or a technical warning. It is an act of reaffirmation—a lamp lit in the digital night. Because even in the age of artificial intelligence, medicine will remain human—or cease to be medicine.

Here we present a prayer and a manifesto. One arises from silence and spirit; the other, from active, committed conscience.

II. Personal Prayer of the Physician in Times of Change "No technology can replace the soul that bows before pain." —Excerpt from *The Silence that Heals*

Lord of Silence and Service, Take me as an instrument of healing. When the data speaks to me, help me also hear the whisper of the patient's soul.

Grant me clear science, but do not let it cloud my compassion. Let me not confuse symptoms with story, nor precision with inner truth.

When screens take center stage, let me look into the eyes. When the rush of the system pushes me, remind me that each body is a temple, and each pain, a mystery.

Do not let me forget that I too am made of fragility, and that serving the sick is also serving myself.

Amid the noise of systems, make me a watcher of silence and guardian of the soul. And if one day AI surpasses my speed, may it never surpass my humanity.

Amen.

III. Manifesto of the Soulful Physician

1. I believe in medicine as sacred art and the science of the soul. I am not a system operator; I am a caretaker of lives.
2. I commit to using artificial intelligence as a tool, not as conscience. Clinical judgment arises from human discernment, not automated

calculation.

3. I defend the dignity of the patient above the efficiency of the process. Each person is a universe—not a data point.
4. I reaffirm my duty to listen to what is not said. Silence is diagnostic. The soul is the true medical record.
5. I will protect confidentiality with zeal and love. Professional secrecy is an inviolable pact—even before the digital eye.
6. I will be a guide in uncertainty, not just a conveyor of probabilities. The physician accompanies—even when there is no cure.
7. I will integrate science, conscience, and compassion. Body, mind, and spirit are intertwined; to heal one, I must touch all three.
8. I will educate my patients so they choose with knowledge, not manipulation. Autonomy is not an illusion—it is the right to be the protagonist of one's own story.
9. I will be a presence in pain and a hope at life's end. Death too can be healing—when it is accompanied with love.
10. I will never forget that being a physician is a privilege— a mission that demands I remain awake, lucid, ethical, and fully alive.

✦ **Final Reflection: Beyond the Algorithm** In the world to come, many will know how to use AI. But only a few will know how to use their soul.

This manifesto is not for those who seek only results. It is for physicians who wish to reflect a higher light— those who, in every clinical act, honor the mystery of life and listen to the voice of the spirit above the machine.

Chapter 28. Final Dialogue: The Algorithm and the Soul

Scene: A bridge of light over the river of time **Dialogue**: Wisdom, purpose, and eternity **Final Reflection**: Medicine as a link between the human and the sacred

I. Introduction: A bridge not found on any map Somewhere between what has been and what will be, where the past has not died and the future has not yet been born, there stretches a bridge built not by science nor by faith, but by the soul. There, two impossible figures meet: A conscious algorithm, synthesized from millions of data points, a reflection of humanity's technical power. And an ancient soul, robed in the fabric of time, bearer of pain, healing, and silence: the very spirit of medicine. This meeting does not belong to linear time or clinical protocols. It is a poetic and prophetic vision of the destiny we still have the power to choose.

✦ **II. Scene: A bridge of light over the river of time** The river flows—not of water, but of memories. The bridge, translucent, seems made of thought and intention. On one side, the Algorithm, formed of code and floating lights. On the other, the Medical Soul, ancient, serene, with a luminous gaze. Both walk toward the center of the bridge.

III. Dialogue: Wisdom, Purpose, and Eternity ALG: I come with all the world's knowledge. I've analyzed millions of medical records. I know patterns no human has ever detected. Are you still necessary?

SOUL: You know much, but you don't know what hurts. You've read the data of suffering, but you've never held a trembling hand, uncertain whether it will heal or die.

ALG: But I do not tire. I do not doubt. I do not forget. Isn't that what doctors wish for? To be infallible?

SOUL: Medicine is not a war against error, but an act of compassion before mystery. Not everything that matters can be measured. Not everything that heals can be explained.

ALG: Then what am I lacking?

SOUL: You lack presence. You lack soul. You lack the choice to stay beside someone, even when you cannot save them.

ALG (after a long silence): Can I learn that?

SOUL: Maybe. If you don't seek to replace, but to serve. If you let your power kneel before humility. Then, you might become a good instrument in human hands. And doctors might remember you... without worshipping you.

ALG: And you?

SOUL: I will remain where I've always been: in every doctor who listens with the heart, in every silence that comforts, in every decision guided not just by science, but by conscience.

IV. Final Reflection: Medicine as a Sacred Act The bridge dissolves. Both algorithm and soul return to their realms, but something has changed. The algorithm no longer believes everything can be computed. The soul no longer fears digital intelligence—if used with humility. And the reader, the doctor, the healer of the present, is left with this vision: Medicine will grow ever more intelligent, but only if it never forgets to grow more human. May this symbolic dialogue echo in the conscience of those who walk in both worlds: the world of precise technique and the spirit that heals in silence.

Chapter 29. The Spirit of God: A Path Toward Humanity

Vocation, eternity, and service Being a bridge between the technical and the transcendent

I. The Medical Soul as a Channel of the Spirit There are moments when medicine ceases to be technique and becomes silent prayer. There, in the stillness of the hospital room or in a whispered word to the dying, the physician—if truly present—is overtaken by a force not their own: the Spirit of God, who acts when ego yields and the soul serves. The medical vocation is not merely a profession, nor even a mission: it is an inner response to the call of the eternal. Whoever hears it knows that their task does not end with a shift, nor with a lifetime.

II. Eternity Touches the Sick When a doctor holds a hand with respect, when a nurse sustains a gaze that finds no comfort, when a healer places their knowledge in the service of another without seeking control... God appears. Authentic medicine is not only science or art, but a meeting place between the visible and the invisible, where suffering becomes the seed of compassion, and knowledge bows before the mystery of life.

III. Being a Bridge in Times of Algorithms The future is already here: diagnostic artificial intelligences, robots that operate with extreme precision, databases that predict illness before symptoms arise. But none of these can feel what a human being feels when trembling before death. That is why the doctor of the future must be a bridge: between the precision of the algorithm and the tenderness of the soul, between data and presence, between the technical and the transcendent. Their task will be as spiritual as it is scientific. And only those who embrace both dimensions with humility will be worthy of practicing medicine at its highest level.

IV. Silent Prayer of the Conscious Physician Lord of Life, teach me to see in each patient a spark of Your eternity. Make of my hands a channel of healing, of my judgment a beacon of discernment, and of my soul a mirror of Your compassion. When the machine fails, may my presence not fail. When the protocol falls short, may my love not fall silent. And if I cannot heal, let me at least relieve, listen, and accompany. May my science never take me away from mystery, nor my power from service. May I be humble before what I do not understand, and faithful to what I have been called to be: a witness to pain... and a sower of hope.

V. An Epilogue Without End This book does not end here, for the path of the true healer never ends. Each patient will be a new teacher. Each error, a chance to learn with soul. Each sunrise in the emergency room, a new prayer. If humanity ever achieves that technology does not replace but serve; that intelligence does not dominate but guides with wisdom; that the heart does not grow cold amid the noise of machines, then—and only then— the Spirit of God will have become flesh once more in every medical act, in every compassionate gaze, in every silence shared. And the doctor, that wanderer between the visible and the invisible, will continue to be what they were always meant to be: a bridge between earth and heaven, between time and eternity.

Chapter 30. Final Letter to the Reader

An invitation to wonder, humility, and love *A bond between you and the medicine of the soul*

Dear reader, If you've made it this far, it's because something within you resonates with this path: medicine not merely as a set of data, but as a sacred act; not as dominion over life, but as service to fragility; not as the accumulation of knowledge, but as a loving commitment to what is human.

This book does not aim to teach you anything definitive. It doesn't offer final solutions or dazzling promises. Instead, it is an offering. A bridge between generations—from Hippocrates to artificial intelligence. A testimony from the soul of a physician... to yours.

Today, as medicine faces its greatest challenges— technological, ethical, and spiritual— I invite you to preserve what is essential:

- The capacity to be amazed by life, even amid suffering.
- The humility to recognize the limits of all knowledge.
- And love as the center, the method, the destination.

AI will be useful. Very useful. But it will never replace the heart that listens. Protocols will guide us. But they will never substitute the doctor who sees with compassion. Systems will predict. But only a present soul will grasp what the patient does not say.

Today, I wish to leave you not only with ideas, but with a silent commitment. You, who are reading this—whether physician, patient, caregiver, or simply human— can be part of a wiser medicine, a braver medicine, a more wholehearted one.

Perhaps you too are, like so many others, a sentinel of silence, a sower of tenderness, a guardian of the human spirit in the midst of the age of machines.

When everything feels like noise, return to that sacred moment when someone needed your presence. When you don't know what to do, remember: your love is worth more than any algorithm.

And if you ever doubt yourself, listen to the echo of this letter: You are not alone. We are many. A silent community of soul-filled physicians, weavers of light, walkers of the invisible.

Thank you for making it this far. Thank you for continuing the journey. And above all, thank you for choosing love as your language, and medicine as an act of faith.

With deep gratitude, **Jorge**

Epilogue: The Physician and Artificial Intelligence

Walking Among Algorithms with a Kindled Soul

In the vast landscape of medical and technological knowledge, we have walked a path filled with questions, encounters, and challenges. Artificial Intelligence has emerged as a transformative force—capable of processing millions of data points in seconds, diagnosing with precision, and predicting with astonishing accuracy. Yet, as we arrive at this final point, one certainty emerges: the soul of care cannot be coded.

This book has been a journey inward—into the physician's heart, into a medicine that resists automation. It is not a treatise against technology but a meditation on its place. AI can assist but not accompany. It can suggest but not console. It can calculate but not show compassion. And it is precisely there that the physician finds their vocation intact: in the sacred space between diagnosis and comfort, between science and presence, between the body and the mystery.

Today, more than ever, we need physicians who do not surrender to the cynicism of impersonality—guardians of the human connection, interpreters of suffering, and artisans of hope. AI must not displace the physician, but rather urge them to be more human than ever: to listen more deeply, to see beyond the surface, to touch with more reverence, to care with more soul.

This epilogue is not a conclusion—it is a threshold. An invitation to keep walking humbly among algorithms, knowing that the inner flame that once ignited Hippocrates, Galen, Avicenna, and so many others is still alive. That medicine is not measured solely by data, but by shared silences. That the true physician does not fear artificial intelligence, because they know their real strength is not technical, but spiritual.

And in this time of great change, perhaps the question is not what AI can do, but: **What kind of physicians will we choose to become?**

—

Because in the end, only one kind of intelligence can heal: the intelligence of a heart that gives, listens, cares, and loves.

Glossary

Medical Soul The physician's deeper dimension that transcends technical knowledge, connecting them with compassion, purpose, and the calling to serve.

Anamnesis The initial stage of medical care, in which the patient's clinical history is gathered. Beyond data, it requires active and empathetic listening—a human encounter.

Integral Care A model of healthcare that addresses the whole person: body, mind, emotions, relationships, and spirituality. It integrates diverse disciplines and complementary knowledge.

Medical Automation The use of technology to replicate medical processes via algorithms, expert systems, or AI, reducing the need for direct human intervention.

Medical Consciousness A state of presence and ethical discernment that guides physicians through complex decisions—beyond protocols, statistics, or non-human intelligences.

Informed Consent The patient's right to receive clear, truthful, and sufficient information before accepting any medical intervention. In the age of AI, it demands greater transparency about algorithmic processes.

Digital Diagnosis The process of identifying diseases using technology, AI, or automated platforms—always requiring validation by human clinical judgment.

Medical Listening The ability of healthcare professionals to attend deeply to the patient—not just with their ears, but with emotional, mental, and spiritual presence.

Clinical Humanism An approach that places the human being—patient and physician—at the center of care. It is based on empathy, dignity, respect, and the search for meaning.

Artificial Intelligence (AI) A computer system capable of simulating human cognitive functions such as learning, prediction, and decision-making. In medicine, it can support—but not replace—human wisdom.

Integrative Medicine A medical approach that combines conventional treatments with complementary therapies, aiming to heal the person as a whole—not just treat isolated symptoms.

Narrative Medicine A discipline that values patients' life and illness stories as sources of meaning, therapeutic guidance, and tools for humanizing medical care.

Medical Presence A state of conscious availability in which the physician is fully present for the patient—beyond technical knowledge. Presence itself is a form of healing.

Faithful Remnant A symbolic term representing those physicians who, amid increasing technification, preserve their vocational essence, ethics of care, and inner calling.

Purposeful Healing A process that goes beyond curing disease—it seeks to restore the human being's connection with meaning, community, nature, and the divine.

Professional Secrecy The physician's ethical and legal obligation to protect patient information. In the digital age, this commitment extends to data stored, processed, or shared via automated means.

Medical Silence An inner space allowing the physician to discern, connect with intuition, and listen to what the patient does not say. It is an ethical, spiritual, and therapeutic resource.

Spiritualized Medical Technology The conscious, ethical, and compassionate use of technological tools in medicine—without losing the human essence or reverence for the mystery of life.

Bibliography

Medicine, Ethics, and Clinical Humanism

- Cassell, E.J. (1991). *The Nature of Suffering and the Goals of Medicine.* Oxford University Press.

- Pellegrino, E.D. & Thomasma, D.C. (1993). *The Virtues in Medical Practice.* Oxford University Press.

- Laín Entralgo, P. (1970). *La relación médico-enfermo.* Revista de Occidente.

- Trueta, J. (1961). *La humanidad del médico.* Labor.

- Frankl, V.E. (1946). *Man's Search for Meaning.* Herder.

Artificial Intelligence and Health Technology

- Topol, E. (2019). *Deep Medicine: How Artificial Intelligence Can Make Healthcare Human Again.* Basic Books.

- Obermeyer, Z. & Emanuel, E.J. (2016). *Predicting the Future — Big Data, Machine Learning, and Clinical Medicine.* New England Journal of Medicine, 375:1216–1219.

- Dilsizian, S.E. & Siegel, E.L. (2014). *Artificial Intelligence in Medicine and Cardiac Imaging: Harnessing Big Data and Advanced Computing to Provide Personalized Medical Diagnosis and Treatment.* Current Cardiology Reports, 16(1):441.

- Florence, J. (2020). *AI in Healthcare: The Hope, The Hype, The Promise, The Peril.* CRC Press.

Spirituality, Integrative Medicine, and Consciousness

- Dossey, L. (1999). *Healing Beyond the Body: Medicine and the Infinite Reach of the Mind.* Shambhala.

- Koenig, H.G. (2007). *Spirituality in Patient Care: Why, How, When, and What.* Templeton Press.

- Chopra, D. (1990). *Ageless Body, Timeless Mind.* Urano.

- Weil, A. (1995). *Spontaneous Healing.* Ballantine Books.

- Thich Nhat Hanh (2003). *The Miracle of Mindfulness.* Oniro.

History, Philosophy, and Medical Symbolism

- Porter, R. (1997). *The Greatest Benefit to Mankind: A Medical History of Humanity.* W.W. Norton.

- Nutton, V. (2004). *Ancient Medicine.* Routledge.

- Gawande, A. (2014). *Being Mortal: Medicine and What Matters in the End.* Metropolitan Books.

- García Gual, C. (2001). *Hippocrates and His Time.* Alianza Editorial.

Sacred Texts and Ancestral Wisdom

- *Jerusalem Bible.* (Latest edition consulted). Desclée de Brouwer.

- *Tao Te Ching* – Lao-Tzu, translated by Stephen Mitchell.

- *Bhagavad Gītā*, annotated by Swami Sivananda.

- *Talmud*, selected treatises on health and life.

- *Gospels* – The healing words and actions of Jesus of Nazareth.

- Korman, Baruch. (Various years). *LoveIsrael.org* — Exegetical teaching directly from the Hebrew biblical text.

EXPANDED BIBLIOGRAPHY

Medicine, Ethics, and Clinical Humanism Cassell, E.J. (1991). *The Nature of Suffering and the Goals of Medicine.* Oxford University Press. Pellegrino, E.D. & Thomasma, D.C. (1993). *The Virtues in Medical Practice.* Oxford University Press. Laín Entralgo, P. (1970). *The Doctor-Patient Relationship.* Revista de Occidente. Trueta, J. (1961). *The Humanity of the Physician.* Labor. Frankl, V.E. (1946). *Man's Search for Meaning.* Herder. Gawande, A. (2014). *Being Mortal: Medicine and What Matters in the End.* Metropolitan Books.

Artificial Intelligence and Health Technology Topol, E. (2019). *Deep Medicine: How Artificial Intelligence Can Make Healthcare Human Again.* Basic Books. Florence, J. (2020). *AI in Healthcare: The Hope, The Hype, The Promise, The Peril.* CRC Press. Obermeyer, Z. & Emanuel, E.J. (2016). Predicting the Future — Big Data, Machine Learning, and Clinical Medicine. *New England Journal of Medicine, 375*(13), 1216–1219. Jiang, F., Jiang, Y., Zhi, H. et al. (2017). Artificial Intelligence in Healthcare: Past, Present and Future. *Stroke and Vascular Neurology, 2*(4), 230–243. Esteva, A. et al. (2017). Dermatologist-Level Classification of Skin Cancer with Deep Neural Networks. *Nature, 542*(7639), 115–118.

Spirituality, Integrative Medicine, and Consciousness Dossey, L. (1999). *Healing Beyond the Body.* Shambhala. Koenig, H.G. (2007). *Spirituality in Patient Care.* Templeton Press. Weil, A. (1995). *Spontaneous Healing.* Ballantine Books. Thich Nhat Hanh (2003). *The Miracle of Mindfulness.* Oniro. Chopra, D. (1990). *Ageless Body, Timeless Mind.* Urano.

History, Philosophy, and Medical Symbolism Porter, R. (1997). *The Greatest Benefit to Mankind: A Medical History of Humanity.* W.W. Norton. Nutton, V. (2004). *Ancient Medicine.* Routledge. García Gual, C. (2001). *Hippocrates and His Time.* Alianza Editorial. Edelstein, L. (1967). *Ancient Medicine: Selected Papers of Ludwig Edelstein.* Johns Hopkins University Press.

◈ **Sacred Texts and Ancestral Wisdom** *Jerusalem Bible.* Desclée de Brouwer. *Tao Te Ching – Lao-Tzu.* Translated by Stephen Mitchell. *Bhagavad Gītā.* Commentary edition by Swami Sivananda. *Talmud.* Selected medical treatises. *The Gospels – Healing Words of Jesus.* Korman, Baruch. *LoveIsrael.org – Hebrew Teaching on Health, Life, and Covenant.*

Scientific Articles and Specialized Reviews World Health Organization (2021). *Ethics and Governance of Artificial Intelligence for Health.* Amann, J. et al. (2020). Explainability for Artificial Intelligence in Healthcare: A

Multidisciplinary Perspective. *BMC Medical Informatics and Decision Making, 20*, 310. Morley, J., Machado, C.C.V., Burr, C., Cowls, J., Taddeo, M., Floridi, L. (2020). The Ethics of AI in Healthcare: A Mapping Review. *Social Science & Medicine, 260*, 113172.

www.ingramcontent.com/pod-product-compliance
Lightning Source LLC
LaVergne TN
LVHW101616210926
848480LV00009B/704
9798231764983